THE RAID

THE RAID

By Matt Gryta

Getzville Grove Press, Ltd.
TOLEDO, OHIO

First Publication 2020

Getzville Grove Press, Ltd.
www.getzvillegrove.com

Cover Design Studiosansnom.com
Book Layout ©2013 BookDesignTemplates.com

Ordering Information:
Quantity sales. Special discounts are available on quantity purchases. For details, contact orders@getzvillegrove.com.

THE Raid/Matt Gryta. -- 1st ed.
ISBN 978-0-9911057-5-5

Prologue

By a fluke of law enforcement luck, the existence of the American Mafia was nationally exposed in 1957 after decades of criminal activity that functioned under the eyes of both the FBI and numerous law enforcement agencies.

With little encouragement from his superiors in Albany, Sgt. Edgar Croswell of the New York State Police Bureau of Criminal Investigation put together within hours the elements of the raid that alerted the nation to the true size of that criminal brotherhood.

CHAPTER ONE

Designer Shoes & Expensive Suits

A group of well-dressed men showed up at the Apalachin elementary school just east of Oswego within hours of the New York State Police raid at the estate of business man Joseph Barbara on Nov. 14, 1957.

The men, later correctly suspected of having been part of the approximately 120 Mafia higher-ups at the Barbara estate for the raid, politely asked the school's principal if they could call for taxis. Though somewhat taken aback by the requests, the principal immediately consented.

The cabs arrived and the well-attired men drove off, spared the public humiliation of being among the 60 men taken into custody at the 58-acre Barbara estate and in the nearby fields during the noontime raid.

When John E. "Jack" Ward, the newly-appointed supervising principal of the Owego-Apalachin School District, later came to visit the school for the first time he talked about that unusual encounter. Ward, a decorated U.S. Army hero of the Battle of the Bulge during WW II, loved recounting to his four children and his lovely wife, Rita, his indirect link to the law enforcement action that exposed La Cosa Nostra. as the American Mafia was known to its members.

Unlike the mobsters confronted at the Apalachin estate, Jack Ward was a

legitimate American combat hero. A first lieutenant assigned to an artillery battalion of the U.S. Army's 78th Lightning Division, he was awarded a Bronze Star for his work as a forward observer during the critical Battle of the Bulge. His Army citation noted that with a unit of the 310th Infantry Regiment pinned down by a German tank and machine gun fire he left his safe forward observer's post and set up in an exposed position to direct effective and accurate artillery fire that destroyed the enemy tank and forced enemy troops to withdraw. The citation noted his disregard for his own safety and credited him for displaying the best military traditions. He was later awarded the New York State Conspicuous Service Award for his combat exploits.

The Apalachin mob "summit" had been called to deal with the possible start of a bloody intra-family war between several of the five powerful New York City Mafia families each of which had seen top members gunned down.

The session was also needed to come to grips with international narcotics trafficking, gambling, including lucrative Cuban gambling operations and further prospects for "owning" elected officials nationwide at all levels of government.

Concerns that had also recently developed about the overall command of the Mafia nationwide also had a role in drawing powerful mob barons from across the county and from Italy to Barbara's estate.

Vito Genovese

The November 1957 "summit" was apparently hastily called, at the demands of Stefano Magaddino, one of the seven founders of the American Mafia. The Oct. 28, 1957 daylight killing in a New York hotel barbershop of Albert Anastasia prompted Magaddino's demand for a quick summit.

Anastasia, 55, was boss of New York's Gambino crime family. His murder had reportedly approved by the Mafia's ruling Commission, which included Magaddino, and carried out by hit men hired by Vito Genovese, head of New York City's Genovese family.

Carlo Gambino

The Genovese family was then in control of the biggest America Mafia family and was allied with the New York City's

Lucchese family and portions of NYC's Gambino family who had been dissatisfied with Anastasia.

The Lucchese crime family had begun in the early 1920, initially headed by Gaetano Reina. Reiner ran that family until his 1930 murder. In the 1950s it was the Lucchese family, headed by Tommy (Three-fingers Brown) Lucchese, one of the founders of the American Mafia born Gaetano Lucchese.

Lucchese had reportedly teamed up with Gambino crime family boss Carlo Gambino to control organized crime in New York City and he had a stronghold on the garment industry in New York.

Rumors that Anastasia trying to seized a portion of Tampa, Fla. Don Santo G. Trafficante Jr.'s lucrative Havana casino business had also reportedly upset Genovese

Shortly before the Magaddino-promoted Apalachin session began some representatives of Magaddino's Western New York family and the Detroit and Montreal families had reportedly met at the Grand Hotel des Palmes in Palermo with Sicilian Mafiosi to solidify "business" connections.

Magaddino had reportedly played a central role in the agenda for that Sicilian meeting as well as the Apalachin summit.

Magaddino had also reportedly hoped the "secret" Apalachin session would deal with growing rumors of Vito Genovese's spiraling desires to eliminate all his powerful New York City rivals and the mob's "Commission" so that he could adopt the long-abandoned title of "boss of all bosses."

But the haste in putting the details of the Apalachin "summit' played a major role in its embarrassing failure for the mob elite.

The arrests and later indictments of a handful of the estimated 120 "made-men" who attended the Apalachin session ultimately lead New York Gov. W. Averell Harriman to heed the advice of trusted aides and set up New York State Police Special Investigation units to keep closer watch on Mafia activity statewide. The success of those units prompted Harriman's successor Nelson Rockefeller to expand those secret units.

CHAPTER TWO

Junior Comes at the Wrong Time

The events of the historic State Police Raid actually began on Nov. 13, 1957 when Croswell and Investigator Vincent Vasisko went to the Parkway Motel, a relatively new business in Vestal. The owners of the facility had filed a complaint about trouble with a customer who drove off without paying for services.

During that afternoon interview Joseph "Joey" Mario Barbara Jr. drove into the motel's parking lot in one of his family's expensive cars.

Having been keeping an eye on the Barbara clan since the mid-1940s because of law enforcement rumors about Barbara Senior's past work as a key operative of mobster Stefano Magaddino, Croswell told Vasisko, according to police sources that "Barbara's kid" had just come to the motel. He took Vasisko into a room off the lobby, telling him, they ought to find out why Junior had shown up.

They listened as Joey told the motel owner he wanted to reserve three double rooms for two nights. He said the bill should be charged to the account of the Canada Dry Bottle Company of Endicott which his father operated.

Croswell's suspicions increased when Joey B. refused to tell the motel owner who would be staying in the rooms. Joey claimed his father was having a meeting of some of his Canada Dry associates and he could not as yet say exactly who would be using the rooms.

Joey left after taking three sets of room keys.

Croswell told Vasisko "It looks like Joe's having a little powwow and maybe we'd better take a look at what's happening at the bottling plant," according to police sources.

It turns out Croswell had been monitoring the elder Barbara, who allegedly had been known in the underworld as "Joe the barber," because of reports he had been a suspect in three murders in Pennsylvania in the 1930s.

The elder Barbara, though troubled by heart problems, was also suspected of being the chief mobster in the south central part of New York State. Law enforcement also felt, but could not definitively prove, that he had been operating the beer distributing and soft drink plant in Endicott as "cover" for mob bootlegging operations.

For many months Croswell had assumed, but couldn't prove, the unusually large shipments of sugar that kept being delivered to Barbara's Endicott plant were being used in the production of bootleg whiskey sold by the mob.

Leaving the motel Croswell and Vasisko drove across the nearby Susquehanna River to Barbara's Endicott plant.

Finding nothing suspicious there they drove some seven miles to the Barbara estate on the highest hill in the area.

The palatial Barbara mansion sat just off a lightly traveled dirt road with no fences or shielding trees and no guards. But Barbara had two friendly Boxer dogs that roamed the grounds and barked whenever strangers arrived.

As Croswell and Vasisko arrived at the estate about 7 p.m. that day they observed four high-priced cars in the driveway.

After returning to his office Croswell's made checks of the license plates on those expensive cars and confirmed that one belonged to Patsy Turrigiano, an Endicott ex-con.

Another belonged to James LaDuca, Stefano Magaddino's son-in-law. The third was registered to a New Jersey man and the fourth to a Cleveland, Ohio company known as Buckeye Cigarette Service.

After finding through the license check that Turrigiano was likely at the Barbara mansion himself, Croswell figured the meeting had something to do with boot- legging.

That prompted him to contact Arthur Ruston and Kenneth Brown who were assigned to the Central New York area for the U.S. Treasury Department's Alcohol and Tobacco Tax Unit. Croswell contacted them because he had worked with them in the past.

Driving back to the motel as he waited for the two ATU agents, Croswell found that the men for whom Joey had booked the rooms had arrived about 8:30 p.m. but had refused to sign registration forms.

While the motel owners said they had been about to order all those men to leave, Croswell got them to let the men stay as a favor to him.

Croswell said that way he and his co-workers "can keep an eye on them."

At about 11:30 p.m. on Nov. 13 a luxury car driven by James LaDuca, Stefano Magaddino's son-in-law arrived at the motel.

Croswell and a few other agents then proceeded to stake out both the motel and the Barbara estate until early on the morning of Nov. 14. During that hours-long monitoring session, Croswell's team witnessed several more expensive luxury cars drive up and park outside the Barbara estate on McFall Road.

Croswell, a battle-tested crime investigator, had developed an interest in Barbara's possible organized crime activities because of all the rumors he had heard about the former Magaddino aide.

His interest in the November 1957 situation had also been also linked to the October 1956 speeding arrest in nearby Binghamton of Carmine "Lilo" Galante, the operator of a Brooklyn vending machine business and a reputed mob killer.

Galante, who later became a ranking Capo of the American Mafia and street boss of its powerful Bonanno crime family in New York City, had ended up spending 30 days in the Broome County jail and pay a $150 fine. He had initially given officers a false name when he was pulled over for speeding in 1956.

Galante's 1956 arrest in Central New York sparked an investigation of his Brooklyn operations.

In 1958 Frederick Roos, West New York, New Jersey's police chief, two of Roos's key operatives on that police force and Ernest J. Mordarelli, director of public safety of that New Jersey city directly across the Hudson River from New York City, were all indicted for complicity in Galante's crime operations.

On July 12,1979, about five months after Galante had been briefly jailed on parole violation charges, the then-69- year-old mobster was assassinated while having lunch at Joe and Mary's Italian-American Restaurant in the Bushwick section of Brooklyn.

Galante's murder was reportedly apparently payback by the Gambino crime family for the murders of Gambino associates. Bot had been killed during an intense war between the Gambino crime family and Galante and his associates in the Bonanno crime family in the 1970s over control of New York drug trafficking.

CHAPTER THREE

The Fireworks Begin

At about 12:30 p.m. Nov. 14, 1957, the raid on the Barbara estate and the Mafia kingpins there began. One of Barbara's staff spotted four men, Croswell and Vasisko and the two Treasury agents, taking down the license plate numbers of the three dozen expensive cars parked all over the property.

With two of the three roads leading up to the Barbara estate impassible due to collapsed bridges, Croswell had his troopers set up a roadblock about a mile from the property on the only accessible roadway. As a number of suits were observed fleeing the mansion a dozen or so uniformed troopers began chasing them.

As Croswell was taking down the license plates of the nine expensive cars parked in from of the four-car garage on the Barbara estate a Dalmatian pup in a nearby kennel had begun barking.

With that barking ten men who had been behind the garage came to the front of the garage, some yelling at the troopers. Some also ran to the mansion.

More than two dozen Cadillacs, Imperials, and Lincolns were found parked on the property.

Croswell found a big stone barbecue at the back of the garage that was covered with sizzling steaks intended for a picnic lunch that had apparently been planned for the affair.

Moments later Croswell reportedly drove down the hill about a mile to tell his fellow raiders "Let's find out who Joe's got at his party," according to a law enforcement source.

Croswell and AFC Agent Rustin stayed at that roadblock as more reinforcements were called in for the raid.

A truck that was driving down the road about 1 p.m. stopped just before the roadblock, turned around and headed back toward the Barbara estate.

The driver of that truck was later identified as Bartolo "Bart" Guccia. Bartolo (1890-1978), a Sicilian-born mobster and skilled mechanic who worked as a handyman at the Barbara estate. Closely linked to the Endicott area Mafia operations, a law enforcement investigation confirmed he was the only non-made man present at the Apalachin meeting.

Moments after that truck turned around an expensive new Imperial driven by mobster Russell Bufalino arrived at the roadblock. Bufalino, a cousin of Magaddino, identified himself.

As Croswell began questioning Bufalino he found that the four other men in the vehicle included the pasty-faced Vito Genovese.

At that time Genovese was head of New York City's biggest Mafia family. Reputedly something of a would-be Napoleon, he was then reportedly eying control of Mafia operations nationwide.

Russell Bufalino

The subject of law enforcement investigations for years, Genovese, (1897 to 1969), was publicly denounced by former New York Gov. Thomas E. Dewey as "king to the rackets" in the eastern part of the county.

In 1958, Genovese was indicted on charges of conspiring to import and sell narcotics. That lead to his conviction on narcotics conspiracy charges.

On April 17, 1959, Genovese was sentenced to 15 years in the Atlanta Federal Penitentiary in Atlanta, Georgia. But according to law enforcement sources he continued to retain ultimate control of his Mafia family in prison.

From prison Genovese ordered the murder of New York mobster Anthony Carfare who had refused to attend the 1957 Apalachin meeting because of an ongoing dispute with him. Carfano and a woman were found shot to death in his Cadillac in Jackson Heights, Queens on Sept. 25. 1959.

Genovese, in 1962 allegedly also ordered the murder of Anthony Strollo after being convinced that Strollo had been part of the group concocted his drug case and sent him to prison. On April 8, 1962 Strollo reportedly left his house for a walk. He was never seen again and his body was never found.

Also in 1962, mobster Joseph Valachi, who was also serving a prison term in the Atlanta pen, became a public informant against the Mafia after learning Genovese had ordered his murder.

Valachi, apparently mistaking another inmate as the hit-man Genovese had ordered to kill him, killed that inmate. After receiving a life term for the prison murder, Malachi began a very public government witness against the mob.

Genovese died of a heart attack in federal prison on Valentine's Day, Feb. 14, 1969.

Bufalino (1903 –1994) who was known to underworld associates as "McGee" and "The Old Man", became dos was boss of the Northeastern Pennsylvania crime family from 1959 to 1989, reportedly controlled in a lucrative multi-state multi-million dollar “arson-for-hire” operation even after he ended up in federal prison.

An extortion convicted in 1978 sent Bufalino to prison for four years. But in the 1980s he was sentenced to 10 years for a murder-for-hire plot. Released from prison again in the late 1980s Bufalino died of natural causes in a hospital in Kingston, Pennsylvania on Feb. 25, 1994 at the age of 90.

In Bufalino's younger years he had worked with Barbara for Magaddino in the Buffalo area. Bufalino had long been suspected of having ordered the 1975 mob "assignment" that resulted in the 1975 murder of former Teamsters president Jimmy Hoff by Frank "The Irishman" Sheehan.

Joseph Barbara

Sheehan, who had been a longtime friend of both Hoffa and Bufalino, claimed that was true in his 2004 book "I Heard You Paint Houses." Bufalino, a member of the Teamsters Union member himself and a longtime labor racketeer, was never prosecuted for the Hoffa murder.

As he was dying in 2004 shortly after he book came out Sheehan claimed Hoffa's body would never be found because it had been cremated immediately after the killing.

At the roadblock as Croswell began asking each of the five men in the Bufalino car what they were doing in Apalachin, Genovese reportedly politely told him they did not have to answer his questions.

With that Genovese, Bufalino and the other three men got back in the car and drove off down the road.

Also nabbed at that roadblock that day:

Dominic "Nick" Alaimo (1910-1990) of Pittston, Penn. A Capo (leader) in the Bufalino crime family. Alaimo had a reputation as a mob "enforcer." Alarm was a committeeman for Local 8005 of the United Mine Workers Union and founder and president of Pittston's Jane Hogan Dress Co. Inc and the Alaimo Dress Making Company.

"Joey" Barbara, the son of the 'host' refused to answer any questions when he was stopped driving from the estate in a station wagon owned by his father's Canada Dry Bottling Co. of Endicott, NY.

The next day "Joey" was arrested by Endicott police for assaulting a photographer from the New York Journal American who had been sent as part of the team covering the historic event.

No record was preserved of the verdict in that assault case.

Two years later "Joey," a former "sales manager" for his father's bottling company, was charged with five counts of perjury for his testimony about the 1957 raid before the New York State Commission of Investigation.

The Croswell-led raiders had found Apalachin participants from across the county, including New York City, Brooklyn, various New Jersey townships, Buffalo and Rochester, New York, Dallas, Texas, Pueblo, Colorado, Boston, Mass., Shaker Heights, Ohio, Downey, Calif., Gibsonia and New Kingston, Penn., Johnson City, Auburn, Forest Hills, Lido Beach, Jackson Heights and East Islip, New York, Cleveland, San Gabriel, Calif. and Sagamon, Illinois. Because of the haste needed to put the raid together with the minimal help Croswell got from State Police higher-ups in the state capital, Croswell didn't have time to get search warrants for the Barbara home.

Until mob underlings gave them the all-clear, the men inside the mansion, who included Magaddino and other armed higher-ups, all escaped.

But Croswell's actions ultimately forced J. Edgar Hoover to belatedly admit, after decades of denials, that there actually was a massive organized crime ring operating in the United States,

The Croswell-led raid gave law enforcement agencies nationwide their first true picture of the massive size of that criminal syndicate.

The Apalachin raid confirmed for the first time the actual connections between New York City's Murder Incorporated, Detroit's Purple Gang, the old Capone mob in Chicago and mob activities in California, Cleveland, Florida and New Orleans.

Barbara, known in the underworld as "Joe the Barber," had once been a key operative of Magaddino's vast Western New York-based crime family.

Because of the 1957 raid Barbara eventually ended up selling the lucrative beer distributorship and soft drink plant he had operated in nearby Endicott.

Croswell had, for more than a decade before the November 1957 raid, suspected Barbara of being the chief mob-linked overlord south central New York.

The day of the raid Croswell learned that Barbara's staff had placed a $431 order of steak, veal cutlets, ham and canned luncheon meets at a Binghamton store a week before the raid. He also found that order had been rushed from a Chicago packing house to ensure it was on hand for the feast.

Dozens of men in expensive silk suits were spotted by the law enforcement task force Croswell had hastily assembled either running to the parked cars on the Barbara estate or dashing into the nearby woods.

Croswell and his 17 uniformed troopers managed to get 60 men into custody. Those suspects were taken down to his small Vestal headquarters for questioning.

Fifty-one of those guys proved to have police records linked to over 270 prior arrests and 100 convictions. The other nine detainees had no police records.

Also, none of that entire group were currently the subjects listed in any law enforcement "wanted" lists and none were found to be carrying any illegal weapons.

Few were even carrying personal papers and most had wallets which contained only their driver's licenses. But almost all 60 were carrying large rolls of cash, mostly

$50s and $100s.

Under questioning they all claimed to have just accidentally managed to stop to see Barbara at the same time after hearing he was in ill health.

Croswell later told journalist that the supposed good- will visits to Barbara were all made to him "with straight faces."

As Croswell that afternoon was questioning the "suspects," Simone Scoizzari of San Gabriel, Calif., insisted he was a retired businessman and had been "unemployed" for the past 20 years.

But the Sicily-born Scoizzari was found carrying $602 in cash and $8,445.30 in cashier's checks.

It was later confirmed through law enforcement sources that Scoizzari in 1957 was underboss (second in command) of the Los Angeles branch of La Cosa Nostra.

Authorities later confirmed Scoizzari, then 57, had entered the U.S. illegally in 1923 and had large real estate holdings in southern California.

After a subsequent trial Scoizzari was ordered deported in 1958. But it took until 1962, and a series of appeals, to get him removed from the country. He was later found to be living in Palermo.

Some of the suspects claimed at the Vestal barracks that they had come to that south central New York area from New Jersey on the Pennsylvania Railroad. Those suspects claimed they had come just to search out possible real estate investments near the Barbara property.

Croswell later said that his team stressed to those would-be real-estate mavens that railroad line didn't have a stop within 70 miles or so of Apalachin. With that one of them just shrugged his shoulders and said "I don't know why you fellows don't believe us."

Late on the afternoon of the Apalachin Raid a car driven by a disheveled James LaDuca, Stefano Magaddino's son-in-law and three equally disheveled men, was stopped near Binghamton.

LaDuca's shoes were covered in mud, indicating he and his companions had run through the woods from Barbara's estate.

Croswell speculated they had gotten back to the motel in Vestal and driven away in one of the cars they had left there.

But LaDuca insisted he and his three equally-dirty companions had simply been driving through Binghamton back to Buffalo after a business trip near Albany.

It turned out that LaDuca later returned to the Barbara mansion. His father-in-law had remained inside the mansion, safe from arrest by the warrant-less raiders. LaDuca ultimately drove Magaddino back to their Lewiston estate three days after the raid.

Croswell found that 19 of Barbara's guests had arrived at the Broome County Airport on Nov. 14 on the same TWA flight from Newark, NJ.

All nineteen had registered for the flight using fake names which Croswell and other investigators ultimately found were the names of unsuspecting neighbors of those mobsters.

The claims of the "suspects" about why they had all decided — allegedly on their own — to visit their ailing friend, Barbara, at the same time that month was openly scoffed by the interrogators at the Vestal Barracks.

That included the claim of the public respected Buffalo businessman and political figure John C. Montana.

It was ultimately confirmed that Montana had actually been a top lieutenant of Magaddino for decades and had employed Bufalino in that mob figure's days in Buffalo years before.

Croswell was quoted years later as saying of the "suspects" he confronted the day of the raid: "They were dressed just about like Hollywood gangsters -- dark coats, wide-brim hats, white-on-white shirts, pointed shoes and dark suits hand-tailored from imported cloth."

While there actually were some young mobsters at the Apalachin barbecue many of the "partygoers" were 50 to 65 years old. About three dozen of them were also foreign-born.

The foreign-born "suspects" initially had no trouble speaking or understanding English during their brief questionings the day of the raid.

But later in various courtrooms and before investigative government committees convened to deal with the Mafia situation a number of them insisted, with their lawyers backing up their claims, that they actually had trouble understanding English.

Those alleged mobsters included:

Joe "Olive Oil King" Profaci. Born Giuseppe Profaci. Profaci (1897-1962) was founder and boss for over 30 years of what became known as the Colombo crime family. He made most of his money through "businesses" like the protection rackets and extortion. But Profaci for year avoided federal tax evasion charges through his olive oil business, the Mama Mia Importing Company. Anthony Guarneri claimed he was in the business of selling men's and women's clothing and just happened to be in Endicott on Nov. 14, 1957. It turned out that Guarneri was then underboss of the Bufalino crime family of Pennsylvania.

Guarneri claimed during his interrogation that he had just been driving through Central New York when he accidentally stopped to see his friend, Patsy Turrigiano.

He said Turrigiano— later confirmed to have been a member of Barbara's crime family— told him he was going over to see Barbara and asked if he'd like to join him.

Guarneri claimed that "visit" ultimately turned out to have worked out as just an "amazing coincidence" because he had just made three custom-sized shirts for Barbara.

Bartolo "Bart" Guccia, (1891-1978), the Sicilian-born Endicott thug who had been the first to test the Croswell roadblock, was a skilled mechanic and worked as a handyman on Barbara's estate. It turned out it he proved to be the only non-made-man at the Apalachin meeting.

Croswell's investigators were told by Guccia that he had been at the Barbara residence that day just to pick up an order of fish, something he claimed he did on a weekly basis.

Joseph Profaci

He claimed he had driven back to the estate after being stopped at the roadblock because he had somehow forgotten to put the fish order in his truck. Asked what fish he had obtained at the estate, he told the investigators the order was "three porgies and a mackerel." But members of the raiding party who had stayed at the estate reported hearing Guccia scream "ROADBLOCK" when he got back to the estate.

After the raid, investigators learned Guccia became a made-man and soldier in the Mafia's Scranton Wilkes- Barre crime family.

John C. Montana, the well-known Buffalo businessman and former elected city official, claimed he had been driving to Pittston, Pa. for a business meeting when the Cadillac he bought brand new only two or three months earlier had developed brake trouble near the home of his long-time friend Joe Barbara.

Montana claimed he had been lucky enough to get his Cadillac to the Barbara estate because he was sure Barbara would have a mechanic on duty to help with his brake repair.

Montana, the wealthy operator of a Buffalo taxi company and liquor distributorship and a Buffalo taxi company, was only later identified by law enforcement as a key operative of Magaddino.

The day of the raid Montana admitted to Croswell's raiders that he had driven to Barbara's that day with Magaddino's brother Antonino "Nino" Magaddino.

John DeMarco (1913-1972) of Shaker Heights, a Cleveland suburb, it was later confirmed, was then consigliere of the Mafia's Cleveland family under John Scalish. Born Giovanni DeMarco in Licata, Sicily.

DeMarco in late 1957 was already a veteran of the Ohio State prison system for murders, blackmail and mob-

linked bombings. He remained a top aid of Scalish until he died.

John Scalish (1912-1976) had become boss of the notoriously aggressive Cleveland Mafia family in 1944 and remained boss until his death during heart surgery. authorities confirm.

Scalish had joined in the skimming of casinos in Las Vegas, moving into both Vegas and California crime circles with Moe Dalitz. Dalitz had taken over the failing Desert Inn from Bugsy Siegel and then developed other casinos, a hospital and other Las Vegas projects using financing by the mob-controlled Teamsters union.

Scalish, who proved to be a powerful and widely- respected mob boss, also largely controlled the Teamsters labor union in the 1950s. He had served time in the Ohio State prison system on robbery and parole violation counts as a younger mobster. Scalish developed close ties to Italian and Jewish mobs and knew many prominent Ohio and Midwest politicians and judges on a first name basis.

Both DeMaro and Scalish refused to cooperate with Croswell and his interrogators the day of the raid. That resulted in both being the last the "detainees" held at the Vestal barracks. They were not let go until about 1:30 a.m. Nov. 15, 1957.

Others taken in for questioning after the raid:

Santo Trafficante Jr. (1914 –1987) reputedly among the most powerful mob bosses in the U.S. and head of the crime families in Tampa, Florida and Cuba. Trafficante had allegedly played a large role in the daytime assassination of Anastasia as a message to other wannabes;

Constantino Paul "Big Paul" Castellano (1915-1985) who later succeeded Carlo Gambino as head of New York's Gambino family, the largest Mafia family in the country.

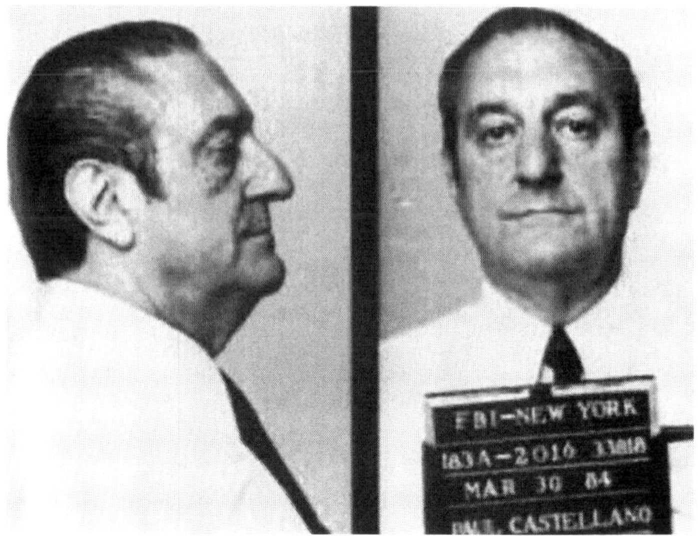

Paul Castellano

Castellano was known in the underworld as "The Howard Hughes of the Mob" and "Big Paulie" and "PC" to his family member. His December 1985 assassination allegedly had been ordered by John Gotti Jr. and had not been sanctioned by the mob's national commission.

Though not captured in the Apalachin raid Gotti (1940 – 2002) took over as boss of the Gambino crime family, allegedly America's most powerful crime syndicate. Gotti ultimately became one of the most powerful and dangerous crime bosses in the country.

Known for his flamboyant life style, he became known as "The Dapper Don" and "The Teflon Don" after being acquitted at three high-profile trials in the 1980s resulted in his acquittal.

But the FBI got his underboss, Salvatore "Sammy the Bull" Gravano, to turn state's evidence on him and in 1992 Gotti was convicted of five murders, conspiracy to commit murder, racketeering, obstruction of justice, tax evasion, illegal gambling, extortion, and loansharking.

Sentenced to life in prison without parole Gotti died of throat cancer June 10, 2002, at the United States Medical Center for Federal Prisoners in Springfield, Missouri.

Salvatore Falcone, also known as "Salvatore Projetto" (1891-1972) allegedly ran mob activity in the Utica, New York area. Falcone's Utica operations was not an independent crime family but it ran rackets in the Utica area for decades through violent intimidation and public corruption, according to law enforcement sources. Under Falcone and his brother, Joseph, Utica became known as the "Sin City of the East".

Under then-existing New York State criminal law there was no valid legal reason for detaining any of the party goers taken back to the Vestal barracks, even on minor misdemeanor charges, because there had been no provable evidence that they had been consorting at the Barbara estate for unlawful purposes.

That prompted Croswell later to tell the news media "It almost broke our hearts to have to toss all those big ones back."

Binghamton Sun reporter David Rossie, who had previously been making regular checks on activity at the Vestal barracks, had been allowed to sit in on the 1954 questioning of the Apalachin suspects.

Years later Rossie, described publicly how as he was writing down notes during various of the questionings at the barracks, he said he observed all those well- dressed men wearing thousand-dollars suits, to a man, act "like I was from another planet."

Rose said those men all treated him during those interrogations as though they regarded him as being "just a raggedy-ass reporter."

Magaddino and his brother, Antonino "Nino" Magaddino were not the only mob higher-ups who got away from Apalachin safely three days after the historic raid.

The other escapees included:

— Gaetano Tommy "Three Fingers Brown" Lucchese (1899-1967 — Close to Charlie Luciano in the 1920s, he co-founded New York's Lucchese mob family. A 1915 accident at the machine ship there he was then working lead to him loving his right thumb and forefinger.

— Carmine "Lilo" Galante (1910-1979- Boss of New York's Bonanno mob family.

— John Sebastian LaRocca (1901-1984) —Boss of the Pittsburgh mob family from 1956 until his death.

After the Apalachin raid State Police learned that Lucchese, Galante and LaRocca were driven from the Barbara estate by Magaddino's son-in-law, James LaDuca; Barbara's son," Joey" and Emanuel Zicari, a central New York counterfeiter and laborer.

Also avoiding arrest were Nick, born Guiseppe Nicoli, Civella, boss of Mafia gambling and drug operations in Kansas City and his mob associate Joe Filardo. Civella had taken control of the Kansas City family in the 1940s.

The day of the 1957 raid Civella and Filardo successfully escaped by getting to the railroad station in Binghamton and taking a train home.

It turned out that many other Mafia figures were driving and flying to Apalachin even as the raid was taking place. They included a large delegation of the Chicago family. All those unknown numbers of mobsters were alerted to the raid and all managed to get away unidentified.

It was later revealed that Melvin John Blossom, the crippled caretaker of the Barbara estate, and Norman Joseph Russell, whose wife was the Barbara family's maid became friends with Sgt. Joseph J. Benenati, supervisor of the State Police Bureau of Criminal Investigation's Criminal Intelligence Unit C.

Blossom and Russell both told Benenati that Magaddino and the other heavy-hitters had managed to avoid the humiliation of public arrests by remaining inside Barbara's mansion with the ailing mobster and his wife and house staff.

Blossom and Russell also told Benenati, who later became the highly respected sheriff of Chenango County, that the autos of John Montana and Stefano Magaddino's son-in-law, Jimmy LaDuca, had been parked in the Barbara barn. That barn could not be searched due to the lack of search warrants the day of the raid.

The Apalachin raid caused Magaddino to lose influence on the Mafia's high commission and he was scorned for months after the 1957 raid.

But Don Stefano, head of a respected Niagara Falls, NY funeral home, quieted that criticism by issuing "assignments" resulting in the deaths of some two dozen mob men who had openly rebuked him about the raid.

Joe Barbara Jr., moved to Detroit after the death of his father and became associated that that mob family.

"Joey" was lucky Don Stefano never learned how his goof at the motel had sparked the raid or he might have become another of the death "assignments" Don Stefano issued after the raid.

Joseph Barbara Sr. who had not fully supported Magaddino's plan for the summit because of police problems he experienced following a mob meeting at his estate a year earlier, died of a heart attack on June 17, 1959.

While the 1957 raid only resulted in criminal contempt charges against 20 of the mobsters caught in the raid — all overturned on appeals — the veil of secrecy under which the Mafia had operated of decades was torn away.

The raid proved FBI chief J. Edgar Hoover's long-time denial of a national crime network to have been grossly inaccurate.

Croswell's team had confirmed connections between New York City's Murder Incorporated, Detroit's Purple Gang, the Capone mob in Chicago and mob activities in California, Cleveland, Florida and New Orleans.

Interviewed by this author in 2007, a gloating Joe Benenati spoke of joining with Croswell in convincing ""Mr. Hoover that there was such a thing as organized crime." For J. Edgar Hoover the success of the Apalachin Raid "was a kick in the ass," Benenati said.

Benenati recalled how troopers had seized "thousands" of dollars, but no firearms from the well- dressed mobsters taken into custody in the woods outside Barbara's mansion the day of the raid.

A decorated Marine Corps veteran of WW II, Benenati described the woodlands seizures during the 1957 raid as having the look of "flushing a bevy of quail" out into the open air.

He joked about watching mobsters meekly surrendering after they were caught, some found hanging on wire fences and some entangled in underbrush in the woods.

He said that after Gov. Rockefeller made him Chenango County sheriff in 1960, the governor used to call him from Albany from time to time "to talk about" the Apalachin raid "and how we ruined their [the mobsters] "banquet."

Despite the national news the Apalachin raid generated, Croswell remained haunted for decades about how the speed of putting the raid together had prevented him from getting legally-required search warrants.

Croswell also never overcame the anger he felt at having been rebuked by various appellate court judges for hauling the Barbara "visitors" in for questioning on that raining day in November 1957.

Prominent Buffalo businessman John C. Montana, 64, had been found in the woods by Croswell. He spotted Montana, dressed in an expensive suit, hanging from a fence.

Identified after the 1957 raid as a key operative in the Magaddino family, Montana in 1956 haven been publicly honored for his public and charitable endeavors through the years as Buffalo's "Man of the Year" by a Buffalo police-linked law enforcement group and by the local news media.

The wealthy operator of a Buffalo-based taxi company and a liquor distributorship, Montana, after he was being brought out of the woods initially claimed he had come to the Barbara estate with Magaddino's brother, Antonino "Nino" Magaddino.

However, under questioning later before the New York State Commission of Investigation, Montana insisted he had really been on a business trip to Central New York the day of the State Police raid.

John C. Montana

He claimed before the commission that he had stopped at the Barbara home because he needed a mechanic because he had been experiencing car trouble near the Central New York city of Owego.

It was ultimately firmly confirmed that Montana, once a powerful Buffalo politician linked to the Republican Party and an unsuccessful candidate for the U.S. Congress, had been one of Magaddino's top confidants since the 1930s.

Montana claimed before the New York State Investigation Commission during its probe of the Apalachin raid that he had only had what he described as a pleasant spot of tea with Mrs. Barbara as he waited for an auto mechanic to arrive and service his vehicle the day of the raid.

Montana, neither before that state panel or to various news media organizations never explained why he ran into the woods along with the other men in the Barbara home as the raid was launched.

To his dying day Montana told anyone who asked him about the raid that he had been shocked to find a big party going on when he arrived at the Barbara mansion. He also claimed that as he awaited the repairs on his car he had stayed in another room in the mansion while Barbara and his "guests" were partying in the Barbara living room.

Croswell told state investigators that after he pulled Montana down from the fence the day of the raid the Buffalo bigwig told him he would get him promoted in the State Police if he just let him quietly slip away.

Formerly the powerful mob granddad of New York's Tioga County and a former Magaddino crime underling in the Buffalo area decades earlier, Barbara went to his grave forever immortalized in prosecution court papers as the "host" of the Apalachin Meeting.

Joe Valachi, the government's top mobster-turned- informant, during Congressional testimony in Washington, said the Apalachin meeting was an attempt by Magaddino and the other top bosses to split up the New York crime network of Albert Anastasia.

Valachi said Anastasia, known in underworld circles as "The Mad Hatter" and who had once been an executioner for the Murder Inc. mob group, was assassinated by two masked men during an Oct. 25, 1957 daylight incident in the barber shop of Manhattan's Park Sheraton Hotel.

Valachi claimed the order to kill Anastasia had come from Genovese.

Valachi also told congressmen the Apalachin meeting had been planned to reorganize the command structure of New York mob-controlled vending and washing machines.

Valachi also claimed the meeting had been an attempt to reorganize the mob-controlled New York City garbage- hauling industry and to discuss the "buying off" as many judges and politicians throughout the county as possible.

The mob informant also claimed to congressmen that Anastasia, having killed his way into the top rungs of the mob's operations in New York City and beyond, was gunned down because of his reputed lust for the lucrative Havana, Cuba casino operations of mob financier Meyer Lansky and Tampa Florida-based Santo Trafficante Jr.

CHAPTER FOUR

A Visit to the Barbara Mansion

ABout nine months before Joe Barbara's death BCI Sgt. Benenati had gone back to the mobster's mansion with a subpoena for Barbara.

The New York State Commission of Investigation, which had launched public hearings on the Apalachin raid on Aug. 12, 1958 expected to vigorously question "Joe the Barber."

It wasn't to be.

Benenati rang the doorbell of the mansion and was answered by Mrs. Barbara. But she refused to open the door. She claimed her husband was sick and she repeatedly refused the officer's polite request to open the door.

The very next day Benenati telephoned the Barbara estate, only to be told by Mrs. Barbara that her husband was both physically unable to come to the phone and too ill to accept service of the state agency's subpoena.

A skilled and battle-tested lawman, Benenati simply drove back to the Barbara estate.

There he began repeatedly walking around the mansion ringing all its door bells and knocking on all its doors.

He finally saw the ailing Barbara laying in a bed in one of the first-floor bedrooms.

With that Benenati began tapping on the bedroom window and calling out to Barbara in a loud voice. That prompted Mrs. Barbara to rush into the bedroom and pull down the window curtains.

Benenati finally got Mrs. Barbara to come to the front door. There she merely peeked through curtains, telling the lawmen she would never let him into the house.

He said Mrs. Barbara yelled out to him that she would not touch the subpoena and that it had not been properly served.

Having survived withering Japanese gunfire on Guam during WW II, Benenati told this author he then decided to just walk around the mansion again with a portable amplifier restating why he had come there.

Benenati said he spoke in a voice loud enough that a fellow state trooper who had come with him to the mansion and had remained in a patrol car parked about a fifth of a mile from the mansion could hear him.

That trooper later told superiors he could clearly hear what Benenati had been was telling the dying mobster through the portable amplifier.

Benenati said Mrs. Barbara's response to him from behind her front door convinced him that she was much more conversant with the legal process than most Central New York housewives.

Croswell's decision to go ahead with the Apalachin raid had jolted into action law enforcement officials nationwide.

The U.S. Justice Department in the early months of 1958 launched what it described as a vigorous anti-mob campaign.

Coordinating efforts of the FBI, the U.S. Immigration Service, the IRS the federal Bureau of Narcotics and the

U.S. Treasury Justice Department officials announced plans for what was described as a campaign against "100 Top Hoodlums," an effort to either imprison or deport the nation's top Mafia figures.

State-level law enforcement officials, through the National Association of State Attorneys General and officials of a number of state agencies all publicly pledged to work with that federal campaign.

That lead to the federal Department of Justice to create a Special Group on Organized Crime to coordinate the effort.

The first Mafia big-wigs ordered deported through that campaign were Russell Bufalino and Joe Profaci. Also, Vito Genovese and three of the other Apalachin partygoers were convicted of importing and selling narcotics.

In early 1958 Croswell publicly said of the November 1957 raid: "From what we know of their activities we're inclined to believe that they had very little time to discuss anything before the party was broken up."

Croswell also noted that "Most of them had just arrived on the morning of November 14th and the early part of the program seemed to be devoted to eating and drinking and renewing old acquaintances. Then we arrived on the scene."

From the motel and hotel reservations linked to the mob figures attending the foiled "summit," Croswell said it had appeared all had expected to spend at least two days discussing family business.

"Undoubtably they planned to do a lot of business, but I guess we spoiled that," he added.

In 1958 the Society of Professional Investigators named Croswell its Man of the Year for what the organization cited as his seminal work for cracking open the secret La Cosa Nostra operation with the Apalachin raid.

But the 1957 raid did not prompt State Police superiors to give Croswell a promotion, increase his pay level or award him any citations for what historically came to be regarded as the Herculean effort he oversaw in choreographing the raid.

Some believed the fact that Croswell briefly booked into custody a New York City newspaper reporter who had illegally stolen and photocopied some confidential documents on Croswell's Vestal office desk got the veteran lawman in trouble with his higher-ups.

Croswell got the stolen documents back, but subsequently his confrontation with that reporter produced Front Page headlines in New York City. Those stories described how he had allegedly botched a chance to keep a lot of crime lords in jail because of supposed problems with the raid he oversaw.

At the demand of New York City newspaper executive various state government departments, including the governor's office launched an intensive investigation of Croswell's handling of the raid.

But Croswell came through that probe with flying colors.

The New York State Legislature's Joint Legislative Committee on Government Operations ended up lauding Croswell for what was described as his "superior" work on the raid.

That legislative panel stressed problems with the raid were actually linked to what it described as the state's legally "Insufficient legal basis." That, the panel's report describes as being due to procedural short comings in state criminal law. That is what prevented the holding any of the mobsters after they were interrogated, according to the report.

The legislative committee, in its final report, stressed that without Croswell's efforts the Apalachin mob convention would likely would have been conducted without notice.

Croswell, belatedly recognized as one of the true legendary figures of New York State and national law enforcement, ultimately was named chief investigator for State Police vice operations in Utica.

After retiring from the State Police as a captain in 1966 he was named inspector general of the New York City Department of Sanitation.

From 1970 until his second law enforcement retirement in 1979 Croswell worked as an investigator for the New York State Organized Crime Task Force, one of the many law enforcement operations that owed their existence to his groundbreaking work on Nov. 14, 1957.

In working on the Organized Crime Task Force Croswell broke the back of a major Europe-to-New York Drug smuggling ring.

With little public notice, Croswell, at the age of 77, died of emphysema in November 1990.

The FBI belatedly began recognizing Croswell, describing what it called his "important detective work" in exposing the Who's Who of organized crime and by having exposed the web of racketeers across the country which had tentacles extending to Puerto Rico and pre- Castro Cuba. Croswell's efforts even lead to J. Edgar Hoover launch an active effort against Mafia operation. His efforts also prompted the U.S. Congress to pass the Omnibus Crime Control Act of 1968 and the Racketeer Influenced and Corrupt Organizations Act of 1970. That stiffened federal laws against mob-controlled gambling and by exposing and dealing with mob financial networks.

CHAPTER FIVE

Not Collateral Damage

The history-making State Police raid at Apalachin — literally The Mother of All Raids — effectively ended the careers of Mafia co-founder Stefano Magaddino underworld associates Joseph Barbara and John C. Montana.

Though Montana lived for seven years after that 1957 raid the former elected Buffalo politician and businessman was publicly humiliated by his November 1957 arrest.

Montana's Federal Court conviction was later overturned on appeal but his highly-covered appearances before New York State investigative bodies that studied the Apalachin incident and before the U.S. Congress perpetuated his humiliation.

Career mobster Joe Valachi during a public session told the same U.S. congressional panel that Montana had appeared before that he knew Montana to be a mobster for decades.

Future New York Senator Bobby Kennedy, a top Congressional legal staffer in the early 1960s, publicly vilified Montana following the Apalachin incident.

For Barbara, already plagued in 1957 by the heart ailment that would eventually kill him, the end came much quicker.

Barbara (pronounced Bar-BARE-a) was a native of Magaddino's Castellammare del Golfo region in Sicily and had come to the United States in 1926 at the age of 21.

Under suspicion through the years for several never-solved murders, Barbara made a fortune through Prohibition bootlegging.

Prior to 1957 his only criminal conviction had been in 1946 for illegally acquiring sugar for his Central New York beverage company. He only had to pay a fine of $5,000 for that offense.

Barbara, a former soldier for Magaddino in the Buffalo, NY area and a mob boss in northern Pennsylvania, had successfully hosted a gathering of Mafia higher-ups in 1956.

Magaddino talked his reluctant former soldier into hosting the November 1957 conference to discuss a number of issues, including the ramifications surrounding the assassination of Albert Anastasia (born Umberto Anastasio) and plotting the opportunities for the Mafia's future growth nationally.

Magaddino insisted on that 1957 summit. He did so despite warnings from both Barbara and his own cousin, mob boss Joe "Joe Bananas" Bonanno, that it might not be a good idea to have all the Mafia higher- ups, or most of them, meet in the same place two years in a row.

Barbara complained about his growing unease over what he described to Magaddino and other Mafia types as a "hick cop,"

Edgar Croswell who had been hound-dogging him in Central New York for a decade or so.

After the November 1957 raid Barbara's heart problems worsened and he lost his lucrative bottling contract with the Canada Dry firm. He died of a heart attack on June 17, 1959 at the age of 53.

Barbara's troubles worsened after Sgt. Joseph Benenati of the New York State Police Bureau Criminal Investigation and later sheriff of Chenango County and New York City Detectives Thomas Fusco and James Burke began pressing him a day after the Nov. 14, 1957 Apalachin raid to answer questions about both the mob conference at his mansion and its possible relation to the assassination of Anastasia on Oct. 25, 1957.

On Nov. 20, 1957 Benenati and the two detectives went to the Barbara mansion on McFall Road only to be met at the front door about 11 a.m. by what Benenati later called "a very gracious" Mrs. Josephine Barbara who told them that her husband was too ill to be interviewed.

Barbara's physicians told investigators that within a day of the raid he had suffered another heart attack, his fourth since the prior January. His medical condition in mid-November 1957 was described by his doctors as "a coronary insufficiency -- not enough blood getting to his heart and causing pain."

Days after the raid Robert F. Kennedy, then counsel to the U.S. Senate's Rackets Investigating Committee, announced plans for that congressional body to look into the meeting.

Kennedy flew to New York City later that week and conferred with state officials about the Apalachin convention.

Barbara's son, Joseph Barbara Jr., the 21-year-old "vice president" of his Endicott, NY, bottling company, was prosecuted on misdemeanor charges for assaulting Charles Carson, a 54-year-old photographer for the New York Journal-American newspaper.

Carson had been rushed by his bosses to the tiny hamlet of Apalachin a day after the raid. Joey Junior kicked him as he was preparing to photograph his daddy's Endicott bottling plant.

As a result of the Apalachin raid the New York State Liquor Authority on Nov. 26, 1957 seized the books and records of the Barbara family's bottling and beer distributing business.

But Barbara's lawyers convinced State Supreme Court Justice Daniel J. McAvoy in January 1958 that the seizure had been illegally and they judge ordered the SLA to the return the records.

Twenty parcels containing the family's business returns were turned over to Joseph Barbara Jr. on Jan. 6, 1958.

In January 1958 Mrs. Barbara, described by the news media as the "attractive dark-haired" wife of the then-ailing host of the Apalachin gangland session, and her son, Joseph Jr. -- described by the media of that time as "hefty" - appeared before a grand jury in Owego, New York.

That grand jury investigation was an effort to try to come to some understanding of why so many allegedly unsavory characters had gathered at Mrs.

Barbara's palatial home two months earlier. Her 51- year-old husband was not called before that grand jury because his physicians contended he was too ill.

January 1958 New York City newspapers were claiming Magaddino and other high-level Mafia figures had met on a yacht off New Jersey in September 1957 anchored more than three miles beyond the continental limit and out of reach of law enforcement.

On that yacht, according to those media sources, the mob higher-ups met to vote on and approve the assassination of Anastasia and lay the groundwork for the Apalachin "convention."

In late February 1958 the severely-ailing Barbara, through his lawyers, admitted to the New York State Liquor Authority that as president of the Canada Dry Bottling Co. Inc. of Endicott, NY, he had violated state licensing mandates by associating his beer- distributing firm with "persons of evil reputation."

That ended his business career as his state license was revoked.

The New York SLA had accused Barbara of having "willfully concealed and suppressed certain facts.... with respect to the character and fitness of the licensee and its corporate officers, directors and stockholders" when applying for license renewals in 1955 and 1957.

Stained by the Apalachin "convention," the dying Barbara put his palatial estate up for sale late in 1958.

The 58-acre estate was advertised with the claim that "a retirement home here would be heaven on earth."

Barbara sought $125,000 to $150,000 for the property that decades later could have gone on the market for millions of dollars.

Prospective buyers were told the 11-room main house had a 32 by 52-foot living room and that it came with a four-car garage with its own kitchen, shower and bath, bar, water cooler and radiant-heating system.

Also stressed in ads was the fact that the ground had a floodlighting system that illuminated the grounds and an emergency power supply if normal power was lost in the area.

On Sept. 30, 1958 State Police Sgt. Benenati returned to the sprawling Barbara estate to give Barbara a State Investigation Commission subpoena for his testimony about the "convention."

Benenati, a decorated Marine Corps hero of Guam. walked around the mansion with a bullhorn describing the contents of the subpoena. As he was peering through a bedroom window on the first floor, he saw Barbara lying in bed.

As Barbara looked at him the sarge smiled and waved the subpoena at him.

Benenati repeated his bullhorn assault at the bedroom window. Local news media reports of that incident indicated the sarge could be heard a quarter mile away.

With Barbara's wife continuing that day to claim her husband was too ill to take possession of the subpoena Benenati tacked it to the front door of the mansion.

Appearing before the Investigation Commission the next week Benenati testified that an Endicott police officer, Charles Wilcox, had reported to the state police that the allegedly ailing Barbara had recently been seen in a car driven by his son, Joseph Jr.

That prompted Commissioner Chairman Jacob Grumet to openly voice his skepticism about the "sudden epidemic of illness" that had prevented Barbara and a number of other witnesses from testifying before his commission about the underworld meeting.

Those missing witnessed reportedly included eleven men who had either "gone into hiding" or left New York State to avoid being served with commission subpoenas.

During a commission session early in November 1958 Grumet said of the "missing" witnesses "maybe there would be a little healthier climate" in the state if they chose to permanently stay out of it.

Within days of the November 1957 raid both U.S. Senate investigators and Croswell had wanted to quickly question Barbara about why so many of his friends had managed to simultaneously "drop in" at the sumptuous hill-top home of the ailing soft drink and beer distributor just to wish him well.

The U.S. Senate's Rackets Investigation Committee quickly began to explore the reasons for the gathering of what was described even then as some of the country's top underworld characters.

The congressional committee's counsel, Robert F. Kennedy, lead the charge, frequently conferring with New York State officials.

At the same time the New York City Police Department sent some of its top mob and homicide detectives to southern central New York to sift through the mass of data compiled by Croswell.

The New York detectives were also trying to see how that "convention" was tied into the Oct. 25, 1957 assassination of New Jersey dress factory owner and Murder Inc. head-chopper Albert Anastasia.

The so-called Anastasia squad of NYC detectives seemed especially interested in why 60- year-old Vito Genovese, another

New York-New Jersey businessman once called "King of the Rackets" had been at the Apalachin summit.

CHAPTER SIX

Barbara and Montana Agonistes

Barbara's physicians put off his questioning for over a week after the November 1957 raid, stressing that their patient had suffered heart attacks in January, February, May and earlier that November. Barbara's doctors also insisted he was then constantly in pain because of a coronary insufficiency which meant not enough blood was getting to his heart.

Among the thousands of questions the investigators wanted Barbara to answer was how the luxury car of Stefano Maggadino's son-in-law, James V. LaDuca -a self-described Buffalo labor union official who was among the guests at the Barbara home — was found in the barn at the Barbara estate.

LaDuca had told the state police who questioned him hours after the raid that he had left his own vehicle back in Buffalo and was in south central New York on a business trip to Vestal, New York.

Three months before Barbara died in June 1959 he and his business were indicted by a Federal grand jury in Syracuse, NY, for tax evasion. Barbara, or "the silent Apalachin gangland host" as he was then being described by the news media, was charged with evading payment of $14,600 in federal income taxes for 1952 through 1956. He was also indicted for failing to report about $38,000 in taxable income for those years. He was also charged with submitting fraudulent corporation tax returns for his former beer-distributorship for 1954, 1955 and 1956.

With Barbara still in his bed under doctors' orders at his secluded hilltop home which was still up for sale, his tax evasion arraignment in Syracuse was delayed until late April 1959.

His attorneys had filed affidavits from his doctors saying an arrest or upset of any sort earlier could kill him because his heart problems had become so severe.

With Barbara's attorneys still complaining, two doctors told U.S. District Court Judge James T. Foley of Syracuse early in April 1959 that they found him healthy enough to make the 90-mile trip from Apalachin to Syracuse for his tax evasion arraignment without endangering his life.

On April 27, 1959 the wheelchair-bound Barbara, clutching his heart with his right hand, was wheeled before Judge Foley as his lawyers entered not guilty pleas for him to the tax evasion indictment.

Barbara, who according to contemporary media accounts, had "slipped into Syracuse with his wife the night before" and bedded at a posh downtown hotel.

Barbara did not speak during the six-minute arraignment and immediately left for the drive back to Apalachin after the arraignment.

As Barbara was being wheeled into that Syracuse Federal courthouse reporters and news reel photographers "dogged him" with questions, according to media reports.

But except for a brief comment about his health Barbara, dressed in a light blue suit, gray fedora and dark blue overcoat, said nothing to the media.

Harry Travis, one of Barbara's attorneys, told the media his client was "in pain' and had nitroglycerine capsules in his coat pocket to relieve that pain.

Travis told the media Barbara had "gulped three capsules coming down the hotel elevator" on his way to the arraignment.

The State Investigation Commission retained heart specialists who examined Barbara and reported in April 1959 that with his medical problems he could be questioned by the commission if handled gently.

On April 30, 1959 State Supreme Court Justice Howard A. Zeller in Binghamton, NY, ordered the ailing Barbara to testify before the State Investigation Commission.

The questioning was conducted in Binghamton for Barbara's convenience and limited to two hours a day on alternate days because of his medical condition.

Zeller issued that order after court and commission-hired heart specialists Richard H. Lyons and Charles K. Friedberg had indicated to him that questioning should be done near Barbara's home with periods of rest in between questions.

By dying in June 1959 Barbara had avoided a possible 43-year federal prison term and court fines of up to $80,000.

In March 1959 New York State's top court, the Court of Appeals in Albany, ruled that seven of the Apalachin "conventioneers" — who had already been jailed the past seven months for refusing to testify about the "convention" before the State Investigation Commission — had to remain behind bars until they agreed to talk.

In November 1959, months after Barbara's death a Binghamton, NY meat salesman testified at the Apalachin conspiracy trial of John Montana and 20 other conventioneers in New York City that Barbara had ordered $432 worth of expensive cuts of meat a week before the November 1957 mob convocation at his estate.

John Sime of Armour and Co. testified that on Nov. 5, 1957 Barbara had ordered 240 pounds of steak, ham and veal cutlets to be delivered to his estate on Nov. 13, 1957.

During that conspiracy trial the jury also learned Barbara had also ordered 30 pounds of sausages a day before the State police raid on the "get-together."

After Barbara's death in 1959 his estate was purchased for $130,000 by Larue Quick and his wife. The Quicks told the news media they planned to turn the sumptuous estate into a tourist attraction.

However, the Quicks' hopes never came to pass.

In late 1961 Walter L. Gardner Jr., operator of a Binghamton automotive equipment concern, purchased the estate from the Quicks for a reported $125,000.

In the summer of 2002 Barbara's piece of Mafia history went on sale again at a listed price of $400,000 for 42 acres of the estate's original acreage.

That sale included the 11-room stone house, a summer house, four-car garage and the barbecue pit where pinstriped guests had been grilling steaks when Croswell and his forces showed up uninvited back in November 1957.

Separately auctioned in 2002 were some 150 or so of Barbara's possessions including his oak card table where the mobsters probably played cards before Croswell broke up the party decades earlier.

Croswell's partner in the raid planning, Vincent Vasisko, was still alive in 2002 at the age of 76. When contacted by news media sources before that 2002 sale and asked what he would be interested in bidding on Vasisko reportedly replied that he had a souvenir no one could touch, "Memory."

Far healthier than Barbara, Montana died seven years after he was flushed out of the woods at the Apalachin crime convention. He died still wealthy, but publicly humiliated.

Famed mobster-turned-government informant Joseph Valachi and Buffalo Police Detective Michael Amico, later elected Sheriff of Erie county, New York because of his actions against the mob, both identified Montana during U.S. Senate hearings late in 1963 as a disgraced former La Cosa Nostra lieutenant. They both testified that Montana had for a long time had been a close-confidant and consiglieri of Stefano Magaddino.

Montana's Apalachin adventure lead the New York State Liquor Authority to launch investigations of his own Frontier

Liquor Corp, which he eventually closed down, and his already bankrupt Power City Distributing Corp. of Niagara Falls, NY. He had operated that Niagara Falls business with Magaddino's son, Peter J. Magaddino.

During testimony before the U.S. Senate's Rackets Committee in Washington, DC on June 30, 1958 Croswell told the committee that when he confronted Montana in the field behind the Barbara estate the Buffalo business man had made "vigorous efforts" to be spared from the list of guests at the raid.

Croswell told the committee that Montana had followed the lead of other mobsters and tried to run through the heavily-wooded area around the Barbara estate -- unsuccessfully -- in their expensive clothing.

Croswell also told the Senate committee Montana "told me he had just stopped in to see Barbara and did not know that there was going to be such a gang of characters as he found up there."

Croswell added that Montana had insisted to him that he was very much embarrassed by the presence at the Barbara estate of so many individuals he claimed he did not know.

Croswell testified that Montana told him "if I would let him go up and get his car and get out of there, he could probably do something for me and he started mentioning a lot of prominent people that he knew in Buffalo and that area and one of the officials of our department that he knew very well."

"He mentioned no specific thing that he could do for me, but that he could do something for me if I would let him go and get his car," Croswell testified.

The hero of the Apalachin raid also told that senate committee Montana had falsely claimed at state hearings in Albany that he had arrived at the Barbara home at 2:30 p.m. the day of the raid.

Croswell told the Washington panel that timeline was impossible since he had begun a roadblock of the entrance to the Barbara estate about noon and never saw Montana's car drive by him.

"He could not have gotten in there after 12:40 and he also told the story about how his car broke down but he said nothing to me that day about his car breaking down," Croswell told the Washington panel.

Croswell admitted Montana belatedly produced copies of bills showing he had gotten the windshield wipers and brakes on the practically-new 1957 Cadillac he had brought to the Barbara estate on Nov. 14, 1957.

But he also told the Senate panel that on the day of the raid "all he (Montana) wanted to do was to go up (from the field where he had been captured) and get that car and get out of there."

Croswell told the senate panel Montana was dressed like most of the other "guests" of Barbara at the Apalachin meeting "for the most part in silk suits and white shirts and highly polished, pointed shoes and broad brimmed hats in typical George Raft style."

When a senator asked Croswell if Montana actually had on "the George Raft attire, too?" Croswell replied "yes sir, top coat and all."

"Large hat?" the senator asked, to which Croswell responded "Yes, sir."

Croswell told the senate panel Montana had insisted to him that he went to the Barbara house well- dressed just to have a cup of tea.

On Sept. 18, 1958 a holdover Albany County, New York grand jury refused to indict Montana on perjury charges in connection with the New York State Legislature's Watchdog Committee's concerns about conflicts in the testimony of Montana and Sgt.

Croswell gave in December 1957 about details of the Apalachin raid, Montana's involvement there and the time of day Montana claimed to have arrived at the Barbara mansion.

Joseph Blase, foreman of that holdover grand jury told State Supreme Court Justice Isadore Bookstein that "after due deliberation by the grand jury, a careful study of the records and evidence before it, (and) listening to witnesses...it is the decision of this body to take no action."

But in May 1959 a Federal grand jury in New York City indicted Montana and five other Buffalo area men who had been at the Apalachin convention on conspiracy and tax charges.

Arrested at his Buffalo home on May 21, 1959 Montana was charged with conspiring to obstruct justice for refusing to reveal the purpose and events of the Apalachin gathering.

In the fall of 1959, the then-66-year-old Montana and other Apalachin delegates went on trial in New York City on federal conspiracy charges.

In November 1959, at that trial, Croswell repeated his account of how Montana tried to sweet- talk his way out of being publicly identified at the Apalachin session.

Frank G. Raichle, Montana's attorney, forced Croswell to concede under cross-examination that Montana had not committed any crimes, including bribery, the day of the Apalachin raid.

Raichle said to Croswell "If he had made any improper approach to you, would you have arrested him?" To that Croswell replied "yes, sir."

One of Buffalo New York's true rags-to-riches stories, Montana died in Buffalo General Hospital on March 18, 1964, one day after suffering a heart attack at his home in a plush Delaware Avenue apartment building.

Montana died an innocent man.

His December 1959 conviction by a New York City jury as one of 20 of the Apalachin conventioneers on conspiracy to obstruct justice charges by lying about the true nature of that meeting had been overturned on Nov. 29, 1960 by the U.S. Circuit Court of Appeals of New York City.

That appellate court held that no crimes had actually been committed by Montana and his co- defendants simply for being present at that meeting.

However, in October 1963 Amico and Valachi both told the US. Senate's Investigating Subcommittee about how the La Cosa Nostra leadership had demoted Montana and dropped him from its leadership ranks.

That demotion, Amico and Valachi testified, had been due to Montana's post-Apalachin unwillingness actively get involved in further syndicate matters. That proved to be the final "stack" in his heart as far as his former mob friends were concerned, they both testified.

Amico, whose anti-mob work made him one of Western New York's legendary law enforcement figures of the 20th century, told that Senate panel investigative work had uncovered what he called Montana's strong ties to "the Magaddino empire" for years until late1957.

Amico told the congressional panel that after Montana's Apalachin arrest Montana had severed his activities with the mob "completely."

Prior to the Apalachin scene Montana had traveled in the best of circles politically, financially and socially in Western New York, Amico noted.

Among the many ironies of the Mafia's cultural ties in the Buffalo, New York area was the fact that as Montana's business successes, through his lucrative Buffalo wholesale liquor distributorship, had grown his business lawyer had been Walter J. Mahoney.

Mahoney later became the Republican majority leader of the New York State Senate.

After leaving the state lawmaking body Mahoney had become one of the New York State Supreme Court justices who signed wiretapping warrants for a secret New York State Police unit that successfully tapped into Magaddino associates telephones for about a decade.

A very busy state office building in downtown Buffalo was eventually named in Mahoney's honor after his death.

Born in Montedore, Italy in 1893, Montana arrived in the Buffalo area with his family in 1905.

Montana was a Republican member of the Buffalo city government's Common Council -- that city's lawmaking body -- for the city's Niagara District from 1927 to 1931.

His mob ties helped him in the 1920s to develop a lucrative Buffalo area taxi business.

Ironically, in his role as chairman of the board of Buffalo's Van Dyke Taxi & Transfer Inc. Montana was publicly honored as Buffalo's Man of the Year in 1956 for his many civic endeavors and business successes.

At the age of 13 Montana had begun work as a messenger for a West Side candy shop.

Within four years he was operating a popcorn cart with his brothers, Sal, Angelo, Peter and Joe through Buffalo's Little Italy section on its West Side.

At the age of 29 Montana formed the Buffalo Taxi Company. He merged it several years later with the city's Yellow Cab Company, development what became a transportation monopoly in that city.

For years, until late 1956, Montana also operated Montana Motors, as a subsidiary of Van Dyke.

He had built his taxi empire while also becoming one of Don Stefano Magaddino's most trusted mob counselor in the late 1920s.

After the State Liquor Authority began an investigation of Montana's Frontier Liquor Corp. due to his arrest at Apalachin he sold that business.

Montana took his post on the Buffalo Common County as its elected-Niagara District council member in 1927. The then-young Republican Party businessman played a key role in promoting the construction of what became Buffalo's historic City Hall.

Montana served as a member of the state constitutional convention in 1937. He served as chairman of Buffalo's Zoning Board from 1942 through 1945.

In the late 1920s Montana secretly became associated with Magaddino and Magaddino's Buffalo- based ally, Joe "The Wolf" DiCarlo, a vicious racketeer who for decades reportedly controlled Buffalo labor and union rackets.

DiCarlo's reported viciousness resulted in him being publicly described in the 30s by law enforcement as Buffalo's Public Enemy Number One.

In June 1960 James P. McShane, a staff member of the U.S. Senate publicly described Joe DiCarlo as a trusted political advisor of Montana beginning in the 1920s.

During a senate hearing that year McShane spoke of the close association between DiCarlo and Montana.

McShane testified that "an investigating agency had informed us that Montana was very closely associated with DiCarlo in Buffalo" at a time when DiCarlo "was affiliated with the labor and union rackets."

McShane said DiCarlo was for a time a power in Buffalo politics and backed and advised the younger Montana in his political moves.

McShane told the Senate subcommittee that in 1934 DiCarlo was characterized by a Buffalo police chief as Buffalo's Public Enemy No. I. McShae testified that DiCarlo and his brother, Sam DiCarlo, controlled pinball operations in the Buffalo area in the 1930s and were among the Buffalo representatives of the notorious Detroit Purple Gang.

In the 1930s Montana became directly linked to Magaddino's underworld business holdings through Montana's Empire State Brewery which operated in Olean, New York south of Buffalo.

Montana for decades served Maggadino as his second-in-command. His links to Magaddino were actually cemented through family ties.

Stefano Maggadino

That was through the marriage of Magaddino's son, Peter, to one of Montana's nieces and the marriage of Magaddino's daughter to one of Montana's nephews.

Montana had formed the Buffalo Taxi Company in 1922 Montana and a few years later acquired the city's Yellow Taxi Cab Company.

In 1929 Montana "convinced" the owner of the 200- cab Van Dyke's Cab Company to sell out to him, making Montana the owner of the state's second largest cab company.

That gave Montana a virtual monopoly on the taxi business in the Buffalo area, with his business operating out of preferred locations including the Buffalo Airport, the city's New York Central Railroad station and area taxi stands located at the area's better hotels.

Montana also ran the Van Dyke Transport Corp., Van Dyke Properties Corp. and the Van Dyke Baggage Co.

Through Montana's Airport Transport Corp., he had a monopoly for years on limousine service at the Buffalo airport. Montana's Montana Motors Inc. through the years provided cars for Barbara and other mafia associates. By the early 1950s Montana's legitimate businesses were generating multi-million dollar annual revenue.

During and even after the Prohibition Era, Montana had supplemented his public businesses with the bootlegging he handled through his transportation companies.

Socially Montana was always a "joiner," heading many Buffalo-area charity drives.

He became a member of virtually every socially prestigious organization in Western New York and served as president of the Buffalo Federation of Italian-American Societies at least five times.

Montana was also for a time president of the National Association of Taxicab Owners and a director of the Ft. Erie (Ont.) Jockey Club just north of Buffalo.

In the late 1940s Montana and business associates purchased the Buffalo branch of Empire Liquor Corp. of New York.

A race horse owner, Montana during the 1940s and early 1950s was a promotor of the Buffalo Golden Gloves boxing contests and a director of Buffalo's minor league baseball club, the Buffalo Baseball Club.

As Montana's political power and his bank accounts grew in the 1930s the former immigrant-boy- turned-wealthy businessman turned to the sport of kings., acquiring a stable of horses including one born of a Kentucky Derby winner.

Montana's wealth enabled his to ensure that his stable of horses which ran at the Canadian track in Fort Erie, Ontario, just over the Niagara River from Buffalo, could winter in either Florida or Hot Springs, Arkansas.

While on the Buffalo Common Council Montana had authored legislation creating the Buffalo Peace Bridge.

That bridge cemented the city's ties to Canada. Montana also had played a key role in the building of the 17-story New York Central Station, an office and terminal building known for years as the Central Terminal.

Montana's close long-time ties to the Magaddino crime empire was cemented with him being present when La Cosa Nostra was formally born in Chicago in 1931 with Stefano was one of its first and longest leaders.

Because Stefano Magaddino was active in the Castellammarese crime family he had been one of the crime bosses invited to Chicago to discuss the formation of a national crime organization.

Magaddino brought with him to that Chicago meeting his own brother, Antonino, and John Montana, by then the No. 3 man in Buffalo mob activities even while he was serving as an elected city official.

Lucky Luciano

Montana's link to the important Mafia summit of 1931 was chronicled later by Joe "Joe Bananas" Bonanno, a younger cousin of Magaddino and a Mafia boss in Brooklyn. In his biography Bonanno wrote of traveling to the Chicago summit by train with a contingent of Mafia overlords including Lucky Luciano and Salvatore Maranzano.

When the train stopped in Buffalo to pick up Magaddino and other Buffalo Mafia leaders Bonanno wrote about Montana getting on the train for the trip to Chicago.

In his biography, Bonanno wrote about Maranzano getting off the train to make a phone call, delaying the train's departure from Buffalo's Central Terminal.

Bonanno wrote about how it would have been "unthinkable" to leave without Maranzano. He said with that in mind, Montana had gotten off the train and arranged to have the train held at the station until the mob boss returned over a half hour later.

That, Bonanno wrote, lead him to marvel at Montana being such "an illustrious man In Buffalo" that he could rearrange train schedules.

"This exhibition of clout impressed us greatly," Bonanno wrote of Montana.

"After Maranzano boarded again and we were on our way, my cousin, Stefano (Magaddino) beamed with pride and said "see what kind of men I have under me. John can stop trains," Bonanno wrote.

A life-long Republican Montana made an unsuccessful run for a GOP nomination for the US Congress for Buffalo's 41st District in 1938. But Montana became a co-chair of the successful GOP candidate, only to see him lose in the general election that year.

The success of Montana's double-life as a key Mafia operative and Buffalo-area business, civic and community leader was so great that in May 1954 over 900 area public and businessmen attended a dinner to pay tribute to him.

At that dinner Montana was given a standing ovation for all his charity work and for his successful efforts to overturn a decades-old national immigration law that had restricted Italian immigration to this country.

New York City Domestic Relations Judge Juvenal Marchisio, the principal speaker at that 1954 testimonial dinner, was quoted by the new media as saying of Montana that the honored Buffalonian "has always realized that his real success in life would be judged by how many wrongs he prevented, how much happiness he produced, how often he helped the afflicted."

Contacted by various media types after Montana's arrest at the Apalachin convention and after Montana had been subpoenaed to testify before the Tioga County grand jury and the state Senate's Watchdog Committee, Judge Marchisio said only that he felt "certain there must be some explanation for his presence at Apalachin, but I will not pass judgment unless I have all the facts."

Just a year before the Apalachin raid Montana's civic accomplishments had resulted in him being honored as Buffalo's "Man of the Year," by the Erie Club, an association of Buffalo police officers.

Montana's selection for that honor had been based on a vote by a group of prominent local officials including the district attorney of Erie County, in which Buffalo is located.

After the State Liquor Authority began an investigation of Montana's Frontier Liquor Corp. due to his arrest at Apalachin he sold that business.

As Montana was being publicly lauded in 1956 for his lifetime of civic and business achievements the Mafia was having leadership problems nationally, compounded in part by Stefano Magaddino's worsening heart problems.

New York mob boss Vito Genovese began pressing for a national conference to deal with the disputes affecting the crime organization.

Genovese wanted that session to be held in Chicago, scene of similar mob powwows decades earlier. Magaddino, then widely regarded as chairman of the Mafia's ruling commission, correctly assumed Genovese wanted to have his role as the top Mafia figure in New York State and throughout the East ratified at that proposed meeting in Chicago.

Magaddino's power in the organization into the mid-1950s was such that he successfully lobbied to have the meeting held at the upstate home of Barbara, one of his former soldiers in Western New York who had killed his way into the leadership of the Northern Pennsylvania mob.

After being released from custody hours after the Apalachin raid Montana quickly tried to repair his mortally-wounded public image.

Montana quickly told the Buffalo-area news media he was only at Barbara's because of car trouble on a supposed business trip into Central Pennsylvania.

He also told the Buffalo media he had actually just stumbled on what he thought was a party of well- wishers and friends of the ailing Barbara.

"I have nothing to hide, nothing to conceal. I can talk to the FBI, the tax people and anyone else in authority because I have not committed a crime," Montana told the Buffalo media.

Montana told the Buffalo media he had known Barbara "for many years...I sold beer to him when he was in the beer business" in Western New York.

Montana insisted publicly he did not know any of the alleged mobsters questioned as a result of the Apalachin raid.

He told the Buffalo news media: "If anyone can prove to me or prove publicly that I ever once made a nickel through rackets of any kind -- that I haven't always made my living honestly and sincerely, then I'll give everything to charity and leave Buffalo."

During a New York State investigation within two months of the Apalachin raid Montana's mob ties were made public.

It was publicly disclosed as a result of that investigation that Barbara had once worked for Montana's Empire State Brewery in Olean, New York, that Jimmy LaDuca, a known gangster and son-in-law of Stefano Magaddino, was a beer distributor for Montana's Buffalo Beverage Company and that Sammy Lagatutta Sr., a Buffalo mobster also found at the Apalachin raid, had once worked as Montana's body guard.

When Montana was grilled by a New York State Legislature committee in December 1957 he claimed he had been driving from Buffalo to Pittston, Pa with his business associate, Antonino Magaddino, who happened to be the younger brother of Stefano Magaddino at the time of the Apalachin raid.

On Dec. 20, 1957 Montana boasted to the New York Legislature's Legislative Watchdog Committee in Albany, New York that he knew New York Gov. Avril Harriman and U.S. Vice President Richard M. Nixon "very well."

Nixon associates later clarified the alleged relationship between the Buffalo mobster-business executive and Nixon, stressing that Montana had merely received a political thank-you note from Nixon for having between chairman of a reception during the 1956 election honoring Nixon.

The thank-you letter was described, by Nixon associates, as "purely routine" and similar to hundreds of others dispatched during campaigns persons performing similar favors.

During almost three hours of testimony before the legislative panel on Dec. 20, 1957 Montana insisted that Sgt. Croswell, the architect of the Apalachin Raid was wrong when he said Montana had to have been in the Barbara mansion before the state police roadblock was installed between 12:30 p.m. and 1 p.m. Nov. 14, 1957, the day of the raid.

"I'm afraid he has got the wrong time," Montana said of Croswell.

When confronted by the panel about why he fled into the woods as the police raid began Montana described his actions as "just human nature."

He claimed he joined in the attempt to flee after hearing of a "roadblock." He claimed he had just instinctively walked "away from trouble," having feared criminals might have been about to invade the Barbara estate.

Though Montana denied knowing any of the "notorious" underworld figures found at Barbara's during the raid he told the legislative panel he had known Joe DiCarlo since their childhood days in Buffalo.

That prompted one of the legislators to say the committee had been informed that in 1957 DiCarlo was "now operating in the gambling and pinball and slot machine business in Youngstown, Ohio."

When confronted by the legislative panel's counsel that Croswell had said Montana, the day of the raid had offered to "help him if he let you go" Montana replied "certainly not," denying such a bribe attempt.

On July 1,1959 Montana's "car trouble" explanation for his presence at the Apalachin crime convention got a rough going over at the U.S. Senate's Rackets Committee meeting in Washington D.C.

Montana's insistent claim to that committee that day that he had been unaware of Antonino Magaddino's extensive criminal record.

That prompted Robert F. Kennedy to cite the committee Antonino Magaddino's "long record" of extortion, robbery, rape and homicide arrests and falsifying passports in Italy, his questioning before a Federal grand jury about Buffalo gambling in 1952.

That prompted on senator to say of Montana's testimony, "the story you are telling me does not make any sense, I'm sorry to tell you. You may tell some people that story and make them believe it."

Just as Montana had earlier told the New York State Legislature's Albany Watchdog committee in that state's capital that he had not planned to stop at the Barbara house the day of the State Police raid, he denied having any crime discussions with others found at the Barbara estate.

Montana also insisted to the congressmen he only had "a cup of tea" with Mrs. Barbara in the kitchen of the Barbara mansion the day of the raid.

Kennedy grilled Montana during that Washington session about Montana's association with a man named Paul Palmieri.

That man, Kennedy described to the senate committee, had been "an important Castellammarese gangster from Niagara Falls" who had moved to New Jersey. He also showed Montana a photograph of Montana standing with Palmieri.

Montana was also grilled by senators on the committee about telephone records of calls he had made to known mobsters in Brooklyn and to Stefano Magaddino in Niagara Falls in recent years.

That prompted Montana to say "I wish the telephone had been tapped. It would prove to this committee that I never had contact with that man or any other man like that."

Montana insisted that one of the telephone calls that law enforcement had claimed was mob- related really just involved a call between his 75-year- old brother who sold olive oil on commission for a Magaddino-connecting food concern.

When Montana told the Senate Committee the brakes on his 1957 Cadillac started bothering him as he was about to drive onto Rt. 98B at Owego and that "there's nothing in Owego but a gasoline station," a senator interrupted him, saying "I've been in Owego time and time again and there are several garages there."

That prompted Montana to claim he didn't think any garage in Owego would know how to deal with Cadillac brakes. He testified that he had thought of the nearby Joseph Barbara home because "he has about 10 or 15 mechanics to take care of his trucks."

Kennedy countered, saying there wouldn't be that many mechanics at the Barbara home. With that Montana replied "no, but he would get one."

"How come you got such a lemon in a 1957 Cadillac?" Kennedy asked Montana.

"I couldn't answer that, but it is a lemon," Montana responded.

Also that day, Sgt. Croswell disputed Montana's claim before the Senate Committee that he didn't arrive at the Barbara house until sometime after 1 p.m. Nov. 14, 1957.

Croswell told the committee Montana's claim was impossible because the roadblock he had set up was in operation before that time.

Croswell also told the committee that Montana had told him he could probably do something for him career-wise if he just let him go home Nov. 14, 1957.

Montana told the senate panel Croswell's claim was categorically incorrect.

At the Federal Court trial of Montana and his 19 co-defendants in 1959 Croswell once again testified about Montana offering to "do something" for him if he would just let him drive away from Apalachin on Nov. 14, 1957.

During that federal court trial Croswell also testified that when he found Montana hanging from a barbed-wire fence the day of the raid the Buffalo businessman appeared to be "out of breath and disheveled."

According to the trial testimony of U.S Treasury Department Agent Kenneth T. Brown when the well- dressed 66-year-old Montana was found at the end of a wooded area near the Barbara estate he was "hooked by his coat to a barbed wired fence.

Brown also testified that Montana's shoes were "muddy and his clothes mud-spattered and covered with spurs and burrs," as he hung on that fence.

Brown told that Federal Court jury that near Montana that day he and New York State Trooper Thomas Sackel had found the equally-disheveled 62- year-old Antonino Magaddino.

Shortly after the Apalachin raid Montana had told the news media in Buffalo that he had only stopped at Barbara's due to car trouble on a business trip.

But during the federal court trial Marguerite Russell, one of the Barbara family's maids, testified that she overheard Montana apologizing to Barbara for being late. She said she heard Montana tell Barbara that car trouble had delayed his planned appearance at the mansion.

"I heard Mr. Montana say his car had broken down and he was sorry he was late," she testified at the trial on Nov. 13, 1959.

Though Montana claimed he arrived at the Barbara home sometime after 1 p.m. Nov. 14, 1957, Mrs. Russell — who worked by the Barbaras as a housekeeper from September 1957 to March 1958 — testified at the federal court jury trial that Montana was at the Barbara home at about noon Nov. 14, 1957.

She told that jury Barbara and Montana talked in a breakfast room in both English and Italian. She said she did not understand the Italian language.

On Dec. 18, 1959 as jury verdict was announce, with Montana and 19 other defendants found guilty of conspiracy in what had been labeled the biggest crackdown on racketeers since the arrest of Al Capone decades earlier.

As the jury verdict was announced Montana removed his eyeglass and could be seen breaking into tears at the defense table, according to news media reports.

Federal Judge Irving Kaufman told the jurors that its verdict was "a most intelligent verdict." The judge told the jurors their verdict had "shown the people that...federal agencies will not be defied or sneered at by those who consider themselves above the law."

Court officials told news media representatives the jury had deliberated for slightly more than 24 hours in totality over several days.

After the jury verdict U.S. Attorney General William P. Rogers publicly hailed the trial as a "landmark in the government's fight against organized crime."

Rogers also sent congratulatory wires to the prosecutors, FBI Director Hoover; Harry J. Anslinger, commissioner of the federal bureau of narcotics; New York City Police Commissioner Stephen P. Kennedy and New York State Police Supt. Francis S. McGarvey.

After his December 1959 federal court conspiracy conviction Montana remained in seclusion at his Starin Avenue estate in Buffalo, referring all calls to his trial attorney, Frank G. Raichle.

On January 13, 1960, Federal Judge Kaufman sentenced Montana and his 19 co- defendants in the Apalachin case to four-year prison terms. The judge also fined Montana $10,000 as well.

Montana -- who ultimately never served the prison time or paid the fine -- was also verbally rebuked by the judge.

Judge Kaufman told Montana, a publicly- acknowledged the former Buffalo "man of the year," he had been "apparently leading a dual life which was exposed by the events at Apalachin."

Kaufman also was quoted by the news media as saying from the bench that Montana "had been under suspicion by authorities for a number of years.

The federal judge also denounced what he called the "convenient facade" of Montana's double life.

As the federal judge imposed the sentences, he told Montana and all the defendants they were not "unsophisticated, unintelligent defendants who have drifted almost accidentally into criminal activity and are bewildered by the operation of the criminal law."

"For the most part we are dealing with sophisticated, hardened, intelligent defendants who have knowingly refused to live by the rules of an ordered society for most of their lives," the judge was quoted as saying on the bench.

The sentencing judge also was quoted as saying on the bench about Montana and his codefendants:

"They have preyed on legitimate businesses and business men and on other decent citizens, as well as on labor unions. They have even sought to corrupt and infiltrate the political mainstream of our country. They have scoffed at policemen and federal agents, even at grand juries. Apparently, they have begun to believe that the law was for the next fellow and they were immune from its operations."

During the sentencing Kaufman also said Montana and his co-defendants were "devoid of conscience and pose a serious threat to this nation's moral, social and economic fiber. They place their loyalty to one another, above their loyalty to the established institutions of our country. I can only conclude that the chances for their rehabilitation are extremely poor."

Montana's conviction came despite his attorney Frank Raichle's Herculean efforts to prove he was a law-abiding citizen and a business and civic leader in Buffalo, New York, who was known for being truthful and honest.

Raichle was also quoted as telling that federal jury that Montana's car had to be driven back to Buffalo by an auto mechanic after the Apalachin raid because of its defective brakes.

During the trial Raichle had called to the witness stand Wade Stevenson, president of the Eastman Machine Co. Stevenson had served five terms as president of the Buffalo, NY, Chamber of Commerce and as a chairman of the Buffalo Board of Safety.

Stevenson was quoted by the news media as testifying that Montana's reputation for truth, veracity, honesty and integrity was "absolutely the best."

As Stevenson was cross-examined by trial prosecutor Milton R. Wessel, he was asked whether his answer about Montana's reputation for truth, veracity, honesty and integrity would have applied on the day of the Apalachin mob meeting.

Stevenson was quoted by the news media as replying that the reputation of Montana who he had known for over 25 years, "was good then and it's just as good today."

Buffalo attorney William H. Munson, a former Erie County, NY, district attorney and a retired New York State Supreme Court justice, stressed on the witness stand that Montana's general reputation was "still good."

But Munson had to concede under cross- examination that Montana's reputation may have suffered in the eyes of a few people because of the newspaper accounts of the Apalachin meeting.

Dr. August Lascola, Montana's Buffalo physician, on the stand at the federal court jury trial testified that Montana had come to his medical office on Nov. 13, 1957, the day before the Apalachin session, complaining of having a cold.

Dr. Lascola, a former chief surgeon at Buffalo's Sisters Hospital, also admitted on the stand that he had once been a business partner of Montana.

Dr. Lascola also testified that Montana, during the office visit the day before the Apalachin raid had needed a vitamin injection. The doctor said Montana was giving that vitamin injection because he told him he was leaving the following day for a business meeting in New York City.

Dr. Lascola also testified that Montana had invited him to come along with him for the trip to New York City.

But the doctor told the jury he had to turn down that invitation because he was treating a critically-ill Buffalo patient and couldn't professionally afford leave Buffalo because of that patient.

Under cross-examination Dr. Lascola also had to admit he was a stockholder and director of Montana's Van Dyke Taxi & Transfer Co. and a stockholder and officer of Buffalo's Frontier Liquor Corp. when Montana was operating it.

Also called to the federal court witness stand by Raichle was Horace I. Gwilyn, a director of the Cab Research Bureau Inc., a unit of the National Association of Taxi Cab Owners based in Cleveland, Ohio.

Gwilyn told the jury Montana was a member of a committee of the national organization that actually met in New York City on Nov. 14, 1957. He told the jury Montana was supposed to have been at that session but missed it.

Raichle also backed up Montana's reputation for truthfulness by calling to the stand Carl

A. Riesling and Miles R. Dwyer, the former Buffalo superintendent for the New York Central railroad line.

Riesling was a former president of the prestigious Buffalo Athletic Club and a former baggage service manager for the New York Central railroad.

Under an agreement with the trial prosecutor Raichle also submitted an affidavit attesting to Montana's honesty and good reputation from Paul E. Fitzpatrick of Buffalo.

Fitzpatrick, a former state chairman of the Democratic Party and a former Erie County Democratic Party chairman, had been scheduled to fly back from his Florida winter home to testify.

But the trial judge had cancelled court on the day Fitzpatrick had been scheduled to take the stand. That lead to the trial affidavit.

After the federal jury trial and sentencing Montana was described by Buffalo news media sources as being spiritually-broken.

Thanks to the post-conviction work of Raichle, a masterful attorney, and the other high-paid defense lawyers in the case the U.S. Circuit Court of Appeals in New York City ruled on Nov. 28, 1969 that none of the Apalachin defendants had really committed a crime by meeting together in Apalachin.

That day the New York City appellate panel, one of the federal court system's top courts, voided all 20 convictions.

Montana was publicly identified to the US. Senate Investigating Subcommittee on Oct. 1, 1963 by mobster-turned-informant Joseph Valachi as a "lieutenant" working under Buffalo area Cosa Nostra boss Stefano Magaddino.

Valachi told the Washington committee that Montana had been "demoted" at his own request following the 1957 Apalachin raid. Valachi said the demotion took place because Montana told Magaddino he "didn't want to meet any more" with Cosa Nostra figures.

After Valachi had mentioned Montana's history as an elected Buffalo politician various of the senators began pressing him for La Cosa Nostra dealing with politicians.

But that just prompted Valachi to say "this is a subject about which I know nothing. Politics was not my line."

Back in Buffalo Montana's wife, Esther, publicly denounced Valachi's testimony linking her husband to the mob as "completely untrue."

Telephone calls to the news media Montana denied ever having met Valachi.

Montana was quoted as saying to at least one local female reporter: "I never met the man in my life. I don't know who he is. I was very astounded when I heard."

Asked in October 1963 if he still held to his claim from 1957 that he had only stopped at Barbara's due to unexpected car trouble Montana said "That was five years ago. I don't want to say anything more about it" telling a female reporter "I have nothing to say, my dear lady."

But Valachi repeated his claim to the U.S. Senate subcommittee in Washington on Oct.8, 1963 that Montana had been involved with Stefano Magaddino's mob operations and been an active member of the Cosa Nostra "as far back as I can remember -- through a good many years."

Valachi told the committee that day that mob lieutenants always "make lots of money" through mob activities.

Despite Montana's public humiliations, including having been interrogated in his Starin Avenue home in Buffalo by three investigators from the New York State Liquor Authority while bed-ridden with influenza, the onetime top mob figure was ultimately allowed to keep the pistol permit he had obtained in 1938 for a .38 caliber revolver.

Montana had always maintained he needed the pistol for "protection making bank deposits."

Montana's physician, Dr. Lascola, told the Buffalo news media several years after the Apalachin raid that a kidney infection that had briefly left Montana bed-ridden for a time in late 1957 was a result of an influenza attack he suffered after the Apalachin raid.

Because of Montana's link to the Apalachin raid by the summer of 1958, his name had been added to the U.S. Customs Service's top-secret list of personnel that had to undergo strip searches each time they tried to cross the border into Canada or return to the U.S. from that county.

According to newspaper reports in July 1958, Montana was observed on July 15, 1958 as being "hopping mad" when he was stripped and searched by U.S. Customs officials at the Peace Bridge linking Buffalo, NY.

Montana died on March 18, 1964.

After his death it was revealed at probate proceedings in Erie County Surrogate Court in Buffalo that he had left an estate of more than $600,000.

In one of the final ironies of his somewhat Dr.

Jekyll and Mr. Hyde dual-life, Montana's funeral arraignments were made by Stefano Magaddino's Magaddino Memorial Chapel Inc. of Niagara Falls, NY.

CHAPTER SEVEN

State Mob Units

The success of the 1957 State Police raid at Apalachin and the unwanted national publicity if focused on the American Mafia convince law enforcement and higher-level political figures in Albany, New York State's capital, that more attention should be paid to that problem.

New York Governor W. (William) Averell Harriman was convinced in 1958 to consider that idea. His successor, Nelson Rockefeller, ordered the State Police to set up units across the state to secretly track Mafia activity.

A Western New York unit of Troop A of the State Police, which had for years operated out of Athol Springs, near Buffalo, was ordered by higher-ups to relocate to Buffalo.

In 1964, that unit which for years had monitored illegal gambling operations in Western New York was renamed the Buffalo Special Investigations Unit.

The unit was secretly assigned to monitor operations of Stefano Magaddino's mob empire and house in an abandoned furnace building at the rear of the Buffalo Psychiatric Center complex at Elmwood and Forest avenues.

Even into the 21st century the Elmwood Avenue entrance to that site that once housed the New York Asylum for the Insane is fronted by the majestic twin teal-topped Romanesque-style towers designed by renowned 19th century architect Henry Hobson Richardson.

The imposing Buffalo facility had been designed by Richardson to complement Buffalo landscaping designed by Frederick Law Olmsted and Calvert Vaux.

Olmsted launched both the Buffalo park system and New York City's magnificent Central Park complex with architect and landscape engineer Vaux.

Work on the over 100-acre complex at Elmwood and Forest began in 1872. In1880 it became a then-state-of-the-art 600-bed New York State Asylum for the insane.

At the Buffalo site while the state Asylum was still in existence a working farm was operated on the northern portion of the grounds.

That farm, which eventually became the site of Buffalo State College, provided both work and food for patients at the insane asylum.

The working farm was based on the ideas of Dr. Thomas Story Kirkbride who felt the insane could be better treated in environments that gave patients a chance to experience a sense of purpose in a comfortable, quiet, safe, and beautiful place.

By the start of the 21st century the Richardson Towers were part of the Richardson-Olmsted complex. The towers remain graceful reminders of the Queen City's 19th Century elegance.

The site is now known as Hotel Henry, a hotel and conference center, which retains the ideas of Richardson to provide a fresh and pleasant side for guests and visitors.

For almost a decade in the mid-20th Century a highly-motivated team of New York State Police investigators labored away in an abandoned laundry -- Building No. 25 -- behind the Towers on the asylum grounds.

That unit telephonically bored its way 24 hours, seven days a week into the belly of the beast that was Stefano Magaddino's ARM, the name of his long-thriving criminal empire.

Building 25, an abandoned laundry building, was at the back of the complex. That building was deliberately left with a deteriorated look on the outside by the state police unit so it would not draw attention to the work underway inside.

The state police operation at Building 25 was ultimately closed in the early 1970s without a public explanation by State Police higherups.

For nearly a decade that State Police unit's staff overheard telephone talks among Magaddino's higher-ups about their doings as far north as Toronto, south through northwestern Pennsylvania, east to Utica in central New York and west to near Cleveland where another mob family was in control.

In sharp contrast, the FBI ultimately failed it its quest to ensure that Magaddino would die in a federal prison.

The FBI ultimately ended up with egg on its face with some 76,000 pages of that federal agency's wiretaps of alleged Western New York mob telephone calls quashed by a Federal Court judge in Buffalo.

Though the FBI challenged that Buffalo judge's ruling that jurist was ultimately upheld by the powerful Federal Second Circuit appellate court in New York City.

That legal defeat forced the FBI to secretly agree to use the work of the New York State Police unit, with FBI agents showing up regularly at Building 25 to get transcripts of the State Police unit's work.

The successes of that State Police unit, which were never publicly acknowledged by that agency's higherups, were outlined in another of this author's books, "The Real Teflon Don."

Often the FBI toke public credit for that that State Police unit's efforts which lead to a series of successful raids on Magaddino operations and the seizures of substantial amounts of property his ARM had stolen.

The likely thinking at that time was that publicizing the secret unit would have prompted Magaddino's operatives -- many of who had their Buffalo homes as well as telephones in restaurants and other facilities they frequented — to alter their communication tactics.

In 1964, under orders from superiors, all the unit's equipment was moved from Athol Springs, New York, to the grounds of the Buffalo psychiatric hospital complex.

That put it literally in the backyards of the homes of many of Magaddino's most beloved and trusted lieutenants.

The abandoned laundry building at the psychiatric center where the unit was housed was publicly and officially designated in New York State Police documents as a facility used for "storage and the training" of troopers.

Being at the back of the psychiatric center grounds the old laundry building allowed the members of the unit to quietly drive to it off Rees Street off Forest Avenue.

The unit's operation was housed on the second floor of the building, with the first floor deliberately left unkempt so as not to call attention to the police operations in the building.

A new lock was installed on the door to the second floor with only members of the police unit having copies of its key.

The rest room on the second floor was kept spotless and the unit brought in coffee-making equipment and a small refrigerator. Two cots were brought to accommodate the regular nighttime and early morning shifts.

After State Police officials agreed after a while to let the FBI share in the transcripts produced by the secret unit the members of the unit, all of whom distrusted FBI operatives because of past experiences, built a sound- proof inner room farthest from the stairs to the second floor. That was done to prevent FBI eavesdropping on calls they were monitoring.

In that locked room were kept all the unit's equipment and records. FBI agents were never allowed into that room.

Bolstering the work of the regulars on the unit was an Albany-based State Police officer skilled in wiretapping.

That trooper would periodically come to assist in the installation of wiretaps and live bugs in mob with members of the unit, all posing as New York Telephone repair crew members.

At those times a New York Telephone Company installer known only to the unit members as "Red' was also put into service.

"Red" was the person who altered telephone lines linked to mobster homes so that all "trouble on the line" calls from those homes or mob-related businesses would automatically go to the secret State Police unit's office rather than the telephone company.

That guaranteed that all repair work on the mob phones was "fixed" by "repairmen" linked to the secret police unit.

Enhancing that operation, the secret unit had its own New York Telephone Company repair truck which could be innocently driven to the homes and businesses where the phone line repair work was needed.

Every Friday the unit's weekly "harvest" of transcripts and reels of taped calls were either flown or driven to Albany to be reviewed by State Police higher- ups.

Normally the material was flown on the then- operational Mohawk Airline by two pilots the unit considered friendly to their operations.

If neither of those pilots was available the material was driven to Albany by unit members.

The operation of the secret unit was not cheap.

To keep its existence secret, a State Police official who maintained operational accounts on its activities listed all funds provided to the unit on state police budget documents as money linked to a State Tire Fund.

The State Police purchased for the unit a New York Telephone repair truck that company had put up for sale.

That vehicle purchase was officially made through the State Tire Fund and the corporate owner of that truck was listed in state police records as a non- existent company.

That truck was kept in Albany and driven to Western New York as the unit needed it.

A second telephone company truck was "borrowed" by the Buffalo unit and kept on a farm a few miles outside of Buffalo.

A special bank account linked to operations of that secret Buffalo unit was listed in the name of a specific State Police official.

Some funds for that State Police unit were also periodically provided by Erie County, New York, District Attorney Michael F. Dillon, a long-time friend of legendary State Police official Hank Williams. Williams was the principal operational overseer of the secret Buffalo unit.

Under orders from Williams the unit would have someone drive every Friday evening to the Erie County government's main hospital.

There District Attorney Dillon would be met in a rear parking lot and given all the reports that were routinely turned over to both Williams and State Police officials in Albany.

After a time, the Buffalo unit confirmed that a number of Magaddino's top lieutenants met regularly at an inconspicuous luncheonette on Buffalo's West Side.

The unit secretly installed a so-called "spike mike" in the apartment that was directly above the back-room table where the Magaddino men regularly met in that luncheonette.

That device operated for months and provided a number of tips that Hank Williams used to order other state police units to further investigate and stage raids when justified.

Having other State Police units carry out those raids ensured that the existence of the secret unit was never disclosed publicly.

The Buffalo unit developed good working relationships with Pennsylvania law enforcement authorities and the Canadian Royal Mounties and passed on information to both those agencies about Magaddino operations Pennsylvania and Canada

In addition to the homes of Magaddino crime family higher-ups the Buffalo unit also tapped phones at:

-- A famous Italian-American restaurant on Niagara Street.

-- The backroom of a restaurant on Buffalo's Lower Terrace.

--A public phone outside a legendary Buffalo night club on Main Street that was known to be frequented by Magaddino's top aides.

-- A public telephone right outside the Buffalo Police Headquarters on Franklin Street which was used by mobsters who assumed all calls from there would be untraceable. Years after the secret State Police unit was disbanded that public phone was removed from outside Buffalo Police Headquarters.

-- A world-renowned restaurant on Buffalo's Elmwood Avenue frequented by many famed local political figures and many of Magaddino's lieutenants.

-- Two Buffalo homes owned by the low-ranked mobster who was known to be employed by the Magaddino crime family to arrange many stolen property operations for the ARM and also arrange for the underworld sale of the stolen goods.

In the midst of the Buffalo unit's successful campaign against Magaddino's boys the Republican Party nationally was in an intramural battle over the party's 1964 presidential nomination

With that political battle getting extra hot in September 1964 the Buffalo unit started monitoring calls to Magaddino's boys from associates of Detroit's infamous Purple Gang.

Those monitored calls were about efforts to try to get a Purple Gang member out of an Ohio prison where the guy was serving a life-term on a murder conviction.

The calls about that Ohio inmate included references to the apparent homosexuality of the top aide to then-Ohio Gov. James A. Rhodes.

At that time Rhodes was a rival of New York Gov. Nelson Rockefeller for the GOP presidential nomination.

Those mob telephone talks centered on how Rhodes could be convinced to pardon the mob figure to spare the governor's top assistant the public humiliation of being disclosed as a homosexual.

In those days the Gay lifestyle was not socially or politically acceptable.

Tapes of those calls were delivered by the unit to Rocky's gubernatorial office in Albany. Days after receiving those secret tapes Rocky flew to Ohio for a closed-door lunch with Rhodes

Less than 24 hours after that lunch Rhodes announced publicly that he was dropping out of the presidential race.

A short time later Rocky personally telephoned the secret State Police unit in Buffalo to thank its members and say he was "very happy" with all the good work they were doing.

An April 1967 wire operation of the Buffalo unit that was linked a key Magaddino operative generated a successful law enforcement effort targeting a Western New York-linked stolen securities case.

The unit's telephone taps in June 1967 lead to the arrests of eight mobsters for a series of holdups nationwide, including one at a key Buffalo bank and a plot that had been designed to lead to the robbery of an armored car in Los Angeles.

In December 1968 the work of the Buffalo unit lead to the arrests of Magaddino, his son and eight others, including his main gambling overseers. Magaddino and his nine codefendants were charged as a result of a federal indictment linked to an alleged Mafia-controlled conspiracy and racketeering operation in Western New York.

Also in December 1968, thanks to the Buffalo unit, one of Buffalo's biggest book makers was arrested.

In August 1969 the Unit's work lead to the arrests of 19 Magaddino associates by the FBI and State Police over a $20 million-a-year betting syndicate operation stretching from Western New York into lower Ontario, Canada.

In November 1969 the Unit's wiretaps resulted in the FBI taking public credit for having uncovered and having "crippled" a multi-million-dollar WNY loan sharking operation run by a key Magaddino associate.

That was at a time when La Cosa Nostra's national take on loan sharking was about $10 billion annually.

In December 1969 thanks to Buffalo unit's wires Joseph "Spin" Fino, then Magaddino's underboss, and others were subpoenaed by an Erie County, NY, grand jury looking into illegal gambling operations.

Fino and the other mobsters all invoked their Fifth Amendment Rights before that grand jury and refused to answer any questions.

Due to the unit's wires in March 1970 a Magaddino-led gambling syndicate allegedly generating

$9 million to $12 million-a-year for the Mafia was raided in Buffalo.

In May 1970 the unit's wires lead to arrests in another multi-million-dollar WNY loan sharking operation.

In the summer of 1970, the unit's wires picked up word of a big fund-raising stag planned to help Salvatore "Sal" Pieri, a top official in the Magaddino organization, pay for his legal expenses in a stolen jewelry case.

Pieri was eventually convicted of jury tampering and sentenced to five years in federal prison in that case.

The summer 1970 raid on Pieri's pre-trial stag led to the arrest of a well-known Canadian underworld boss who had come to Buffalo for that affair.

In 1971 another Erie County grand jury in Buffalo indicted 44 mob-linked suspects for possession of stolen jewelry, much from break-ins at the homes of noted local businessmen, thanks to the secret State Police unit's wire work.

Also in 1971, the thefts of several million dollars' worth of paintings were solved through information picked up by the secret State Police unit through livening to Magaddino family telephone lines.

The recovered paintings had been stolen from the George Eastman Museum in Rochester, New York, from the Bradford, PA. mansion of the widow of a late oil industry millionaire and from the home of Buffalo banker and internationally-known modern art collector Seymour H. Knox.

In early 1972 the unit's wires lead to the closing of a major stolen property operation of the Magaddino family.

That operation was closed due to raids on an antique shop on Buffalo's Broadway (a street with no last name).

That antique shop "shipping" outlet had been sending stolen property from Western New York all over the Eastern seaboard, the secret State Police unit learned through its telephone line taps. In November 1972, even though the State Police Unit has closed shop a month earlier, an Erie County grand jury — thanks to the State Police unit's wires — broke up another mob-run loan sharking operation in Buffalo that had been illegally charging interest rates on "loans" that violated New York State's Usury Law.

ACKNOWLEDGEMENTS

The author would like to express his gratitude to the following individuals and organizations that provided assistance in the creation of this work:

Daniel DiLandro, Buffalo State College archivist and special collections librarian; E.H. Butler Library, Buffalo State College, Buffalo, N.Y.; Buffalo Courier-Express, Buffalo, N.Y.; Buffalo Evening News, later The Buffalo News, Buffalo, N.Y.; Buffalo and Erie County Public Library; George Karalus, the last living member of the New York State Police Unit that secretly listened to the telephone calls of the top member of the Maggadino Crime Family, who died in his own bed on May 26, 2019 at the age of 85; Dan Ward, a son of John Ward and a former town supervisor. of Amherst, New York.

ABOUT THE AUTHOR

Matt Gryta, a Western New York journalist for over four decades, began his career with two years as editor-in-chief of the Buffalo State College RECORD. For over 40 years he served as a Buffalo News staff reporter. From 1970 through May 197, as a draftee who came into the U.S. Army with professional experience as a police reporter and general assignment reporter for what was then the Buffalo Evening News, he became a U.S. Army war correspondent in Vietnam as a sergeant heading the writers and photographers in the Public Information Office of the Americal Division. That division was the reactivated 23rd Infantry Division formed in May 1942 on the island of New Caledonia after the Japanese attack on Pearl Harbor. Its name was a contraction of "American, New Caledonian Division." Gryta was one of the principal reporters covering the developments in the Trait case.

Among Gryta's other non-fiction books are:
The Real Teflon Don, the first public disclosure of the secret New York State Police unit that in the late 1960s until early in the next decade successfully tape- recorded the telephone conversations of upper limits of the crime empire of Mafia co-founder Stefano Magaddino and his chief operatives.

Joey 22, the full story of Joe Christopher, the Buffalo-raised racial serial killer of Black and Latino men late in the 20th Century.

A Death in Buffalo, which covers the death of Richard Yancey Long Jr. at the hands of two off-duty Buffalo, New York, police officers and their tobacco-salesman friend.

The Four Angels, which covers the gruesome murder case of Gail Trait's four children in Buffalo, New York